just
soup

Lincolnshire
COUNTY COUNCIL

discover libraries

**This book should be returned on or before
the due date.**

MCI

To renew or order library books please telephone 01522 782010
or visit https://lincolnshire.spydus.co.uk

You will require a Personal Identification Number.
Ask any member of staff for this.

The above does not apply to Reader's Group Collection Stock.

just
soup
everything
you
need
in a
bowl

Henrietta Clancy

Photographs by Romas Foord

On soup

There's something comforting about tackling a meal with a spoon. For most of us it was the first utensil we held.

It's soup spoons specifically that I've always had a thing for. As a child I rifled through the cutlery draw before breakfast and sought one out for cereal, the better to savour its pools of liquid. I used it for ice cream too, as well as for food that a fork might have been better suited to. I was in good company with my quirk. The food writer Bee Wilson's tool of choice was a teaspoon: 'as an eccentric and somewhat troubled teenager, for several years I ate all my food – anything that didn't need cutting, at any rate – with a teaspoon … I remember how safe it made me feel, spooning up tiny morsels like an infant.'

Perhaps the comfort of spoons has got something to do with the fact that when you're armed with one you're most likely eating from a bowl. You have a hand free to cradle that bowl, feel the warmth within, and a chance to really consider what's before you.

It's odd really that soup gets pigeon-holed as a cold-weather food, because it's most prevalent in countries where the temperature seldom dips beneath that of the hottest day in an English August. India's thick dals, Vietnam's clear phos, Thailand's coconut broths, Africa's pulse-heavy stews, they're all consumed in the sun. And yet in England we seem to have given ourselves an all too brief soup season that begins when leaves fall and ends as soon as we take our scarves off. If we were going to assign liquid food to any season, in fact, it would probably make more sense to give it to summer, where its high water content would keep us hydrated. This is precisely why soup is popular all over the world, and one of the many reasons it is the ultimate food of convalescence.

Nutritional fads may come and go but soup, imbued with the power to heal the sick and warm the soul, is a mainstay. As well as being a liquid and therefore a vehicle for easily digestible nutrients, soups made from slow-cooked bones also have anti-inflammatory properties. Chicken soup, sometimes referred to as 'Jewish penicillin', is probably the most revered and long-standing example, but there are others, from the rice congees of Chinese folklore to the ancient Ayurvedic soups of India. Of course you don't need to be sick to enjoy the benefits of soup. I believe a soup can be found for most occasions and will satiate most cravings – rich and piquant broths to replenish salt levels after exercise, colourful and spicy curried soups to light up your eyes and stir your nostrils, and tangy sour soups to refresh and energise.

Soup offers health for everyone. At a time when people struggle to meet their five-a-day, soup can neatly smuggle the necessaries into a bowl. If you are given to dieting you could do much worse than live off soup three or four days a week – and 'souping' is certainly a far more gratifying and beneficial alternative to high-sugar juice diets. Soup provides nourishment while helping you lose weight. You can feel full as well as great. And because it's easy to digest you are more likely after an evening bowl to have a restful night's sleep and wake with energy.

The recipes included in this book are not diet soups, but neither are they creamed or thickened with egg yolks – techniques I feel are better suited to small portions, or starters, whereas all of the soups here will work as main meals.

A brisk, kineograph-style flick through its pages will show you I am not afraid of garnishes. They bring crunch, they help make a soup a meal and they are a great way of introducing contrasting flavours and raw ingredients. They also look good. The importance of having something beautiful to look at while you eat should never be underestimated.

Soup's beginnings are humble – it was a peasant food, a repository for the chopping board's odds and ends, but it soon evolved from being mere fuel and became a decadent course for those who could afford it, an agent for letting specific ingredients shine and be savoured. Soup is, perhaps, the most universal type of food there is, steeped in history and yet ripe for reinvention. I hope this book inspires you in your quest to do the latter.

Equipment

Blenders

Some form of blender is essential if you're going to make a smooth or even partially blended soup. Stick blenders are incredibly convenient because you can place them directly into your pot instead of transferring the soup into another blender or food processor and increasing your washing-up. They're especially useful for rough-blended and partially blended soups. If you're after a more refined finish then a jug blender or a food processor is probably better suited to the job. Small personal blenders, like the Nutri-bullet, and other high-powered brands that have recently flooded the market, are as perfect for souping as they are for making smoothies. Furthermore, because most of them now come with smaller attachments, they can be used in much the same way as a pestle and mortar – to grind nuts and make pestos and salsas. For raw soups in particular, where ingredients haven't been softened by heat, personal blenders are very useful for grinding through fibrous skin, roots and hard seeds, resulting in beautifully soft and easy to digest soups.

No other equipment is essential, but the following items can be useful.

Ladles

Serving soups can be quite tricky without them. They don't have many uses, but they do what they do well.

Microplanes

Are up there with SatNav and the mobile phone in my book. Their arrival changed everything. Originally intended as tools for wood, microplanes are a joy to work with and easy to clean – use them for garlic, ginger, cheese and citrus zest.

Mandolines

Are incredibly useful when the user is familiar with them, and occasionally dangerous when not. I use them a lot, even for garlic. They give you thinly sliced, uniform pieces of veg – necessary when you'd like everything to cook quickly (see nutty parsnip p38) or look pretty (see springtime broth p86). They can do to your fingers what they do to your veg, so be especially cautious.

Pestles and mortars
Useful for grinding small amounts of spices, granted, but I believe that the back of a large knife can also be used to great effect.

Freezer bags
Soup-specific freezer bags with thick structured bases are handy but expensive. As an alternative use a normal sandwich bag in a Tupperware container. When the soup has frozen remove it from the container.

Zesters
By which I mean the hand-held instrument with a metal end that has a row of holes across the top. These are useful for decorative strips or ribbons of citrus zest to garnish. Invest in a sturdy one. I think the bubbly-ended Zyliss model is particularly good.

Stock

You don't always need stock. There are plenty of other flavoursome liquids like coconut water, milk, cider, wine and beer which you can use as a base, and soup that contains meat – especially mince, which has such a large surface area it instantly gives up its flavours – is fine made with water. There are occasions, however, when using a stock either improves things greatly or is downright essential. You can make your own or you can buy it. Making stock requires very different levels of commitment depending on whether it's meat, fish or vegetable.

Meat stock is the most laborious to make. It involves coaxing gelatine out of bones with gentle heat, and can take anything between 2 hours (chicken) to 6 hours (beef). However, it's also the most rewarding because you get texture from your stock as well as flavour. A stock cube will give you some deep, meaty undertones (often not as subtle as you'd like) but it won't provide the gelatine reputed to have such marvellous healing qualities. Making meat stock is a great habit to get into, but if you haven't the time then pre-made pouches are a fine alternative. Always taste before using as occasionally these pouches are over-salted.

Fish stock is worth making for the same reasons, as the process extracts gelatine from the bones, though to a lesser extent. It's a much shorter process, 2 hours being plenty to get you what you need. Again pre-made pouches are lifesavers, but note that these tend to contain shellfish, which gives everything a bisque flavour.

Vegetable stock is both quick and easy. Vegetables and spices are resilient and will generously give up their flavours in 30 minutes in some briskly bubbling water. An onion, a carrot, a stick of celery and some hardy herbs will get you far. Adding a piece of lemon skin, a smashed garlic clove and some crushed spices will get you even farther. I have suggested a list of ingredients that you might like to use in a quick veg stock beside each relevant recipe.

I'm not entirely against using instant vegetable stocks. They can work well, but their heavily herby flavour can wreck some delicately flavoured soups. If you're making your own quick veg stock and feeling it's lacking oomph, you can always add a pinch of Marigold's bouillon powder, or the corner of a stock cube, to help things along.

Meat and fish stock recipes

A good ratio for meat and fish stock is 3 parts water to 2 parts bones, which translates as 1.5 litres to 1kg bones. Vegetables and aromatics can be added to fill the space remaining in the pot; everything should be covered by water and remain so during cooking. Meat/fish stock should never boil. Either cook on the hob using your tamest flame, or put it in the oven, uncovered, at 90°C/70°C fan (boiling point is 100°C, and it needs to be lower). Sieve these stocks using a fine-mesh sieve or muslin – if you have neither, then a napkin, coffee filter or thin tea-towel will do. Failing to sieve can result in a bitter stock. Cool and refrigerate for 5 days or freeze for a month. All vegetables and aromatics listed in these recipes are merely suggestions.

Beef – 1 litre
1kg meaty bones, cut into 5cm pieces, and joints
Onion, carrot, tomatoes, tomato paste, bay, parsley, thyme

Preheat the oven to 220°C/200°C fan. Place the bones in a roasting tray and cook for an hour. Transfer the bones to a large saucepan and cover with 1.5 litres cold water. Slowly bring to the boil, then reduce the heat and simmer very gently for 4-8 hours. Add the vegetables and aromatics for the final hour. Strain.

Chicken – 1 litre
1kg raw bones, cut into 5cm pieces, and wings, kept whole
Onion, celery, carrot, leek, parsley, tarragon, bay, thyme, garlic, crushed peppercorns, lemon peel

Place the bones and wings in a large saucepan and cover with 1.5 litres

water. Bring to the boil and skim the surface (if you are using a cooked chicken carcass instead of raw bones, you won't need to bother with the skimming stage). Reduce the heat and simmer very gently for 2-4 hours. Add the vegetables and aromatics for the final hour. Strain.

Ham hock stock – 1 litre
1 small ham hock, about 1kg
Onion, celery, carrot, leek, bay, thyme, crushed peppercorns

Put the hock in a large saucepan and cover with cold water. Bring slowly to the boil. Pour the water away and rinse the ham and saucepan. Cover with 1.5 litres of cold water. Bring to the boil and skim the surface. Reduce the heat and simmer very gently for 3 hours. Add the vegetables and aromatics for the final hour. Strain, and reserve meat.

Fish stock – 1 litre
1kg bones from white-fleshed fish (seabass, sole, turbot)
Onion, carrot, celery, fennel, tarragon, bay, thyme, parsley

Put the bones in a large saucepan and cover with 1.5 litres cold water. Add the vegetables and aromatics and slowly bring to the boil. Skim the surface. Reduce the heat and simmer very gently for 1 hour. Strain.

Veg stock recipe – quick/all-purpose – 1 litre
The same ratio applies to vegetable stocks: 1.5 litres to 1kg vegetables.

1kg chopped vegetables: leeks, carrots, celery and any other vegetable relevant to the soup in question
tarragon, bay, thyme, parsley, lemon peel, garlic, according to taste

Chop the vegetables into 2cm pieces. Place in a large saucepan with the aromatics and cover with 1.5 litres cold water. Bring to the boil then continue to boil rapidly for 30 minutes. Strain.

Practicalities

Portions

All of these recipes are for two, a number that is easily halved or multiplied. They are intended as main courses (that don't rely on a side of bread) but servings are a rather personal thing so if you're worried make more, especially as your soup will often taste better the next day. Unless otherwise stated, all soups keep for two days in the fridge.

Freezing

Most soups keep for a month in the freezer. Frozen soups can look particularly homogenous, though, so if left unlabelled they will become lucky dip meals. This is no bad thing if you like everything you make!

Soups that freeze well

Those made with:

pulses	blended or otherwise
meat	mince or chunks
vegetables	puréed
rice	

Soups to avoid freezing

Those containing:

a lot of dairy	they separate and the texture goes from creamy to mealy
seafood soups	they lose their flavour and the flesh can take on a spongy texture
soups thickened with cornflour	they become watery
potato heavy soups	they change texture and become grainy
soups full of fresh herbs	those fresh flavours won't survive the cold

Thickeners

Quick tricks if your finished blended soup is too liquid:

cooked rice/ potatoes/pulses	add several spoonfuls before blending
cornflour	make a slurry by mixing 1-2 tbsp with a little cold water, then slowly whisk into soup while heating. Keep stirring till thickened
egg yolks	pour several tbsp of the hot soup onto a beaten egg yolk or two, return everything to the pot and cook gently until thickened, being careful not to boil as this will curdle the eggs
flour	make a slurry by adding water, as with cornflour above, or make beurre manié, which is a dough of equal parts soft butter and flour whisked into the hot liquid
lentils	grind 1 tbsp in a blender and add to pot; heat and stir until thickened
nuts	1 tbsp of ground nuts can be added directly to the pot, buy them ready-ground, grind your own or simply use a tbsp of nut butter
oats	grind 1 tbsp in a blender and add to the pot, heat and stir until thickened
polenta	add 1 tbsp to the pot, heat and stir until thickened

Problem solving

Your soup is:

too thick	add more stock, milk or any other relevant liquid; watery ingredients like tomatoes will help too. You'll need to adjust your seasoning
too bland	add salt, often you need more than you think. If this doesn't improve matters turn to the other four basic tastes; sweetness, sourness, bitterness and umami – a squeeze of lemon and a spoon tip of honey are often enough to help things along
too salty	add more of the original ingredients, or dairy, starch, a little sugar
too sweet	add salt and a little sourness from lemon or vinegar
too thin	see thickeners
too sour	sieve in a scant tsp of baking soda to neutralise the acid

Noteworthy ingredients

Cheese

Cheddar	a tangy number that grated on top complements many a smooth soup
feta	unapologetically salty, especially good with tomato-based soups
Parmesan	a hard Italian cow's milk cheese, delicious grated on top of soups; also has a useful rind for flavouring stocks
pecorino	Parmesan's lesser-known sibling from the Italian south, a sheep's milk cheese, nuttier and slightly rubbery, in a good way.

Citrus

lemon	provides high acidity, enlivens the vast majority of soups from the tomato-based to the lentil-heavy
lime	is a touch more bitter and perfumed than its bigger brother, well suited to finishing Asian broths, where it goes well with kaffir leaves and ginger
orange	lacks the harsh acidity of lemon and lime but brings a unique sweetness
zest	releases zingy oils. Use a zester to get larger strips of citrus which are useful for imparting more obvious flavours

Dairy

cream	a small swirl to finish a soup has a big effect
crème fraîche	always decadent, even when half-fat, with underlying tang
sour cream	as the name suggests, sour; a slightly bitter, thickened cream which is marginally lighter than crème fraîche
yoghurt	a milk product rather than a cream product like those above and therefore often lower in fat

Herbs

bay	always added at the beginning, usually with liquid, never used as a garnish; it's easy to forget bay as its potency isn't immediately apparent, but its soft underlying spice accounts for a lot in most stocks and a great deal of soups
chives	add a delicate whiff of onion to a finished dish when snipped on top, at a stretch can be used as a replacement for spring onions

Herbs (cont.)

coriander	I can't imagine life without this herb, never mind soup, but not everyone feels the same: lovers say it's warm and citrusy; haters say it's soapy. It's certainly aromatic, but its delicacy means it's better suited to being added towards the end of cooking
mint	a surprisingly universal herb, sweet, strong and fresh with a cool aftertaste, it sits happily in pea soup and pho
parsley	possesses a brilliant bitterness which is adept at toning down overly sweet soups, like those made with tomato and red pepper; thick stalks are an excellent addition to quick stocks
rosemary	hardy and best suited to joining onions in the pan at the beginning of proceedings, an aromatic stalk in a stock is a good thing too.
sage	is so strong that a single leaf goes a long way; always shred this astringent but warm herb finely; it's more commonly used at the beginning of cooking, though you can add with caution at the end.
tarragon	overwhelmingly aniseedy and therefore divides parties; a good herb for flavouring oil and drizzling over soup; also a quick veg stock contender
thyme	shares all of rosemary's good points, can often replace it and withstand long cooking times; however, its little leaves are also lovely sprinkled raw on top of finished dishes

Liquid

coconut milk	tames the heat in spicy Asian soups, tenderises meat, is a great dairy-free alternative for creamy soups
coconut water	celebrity life-giving drink turned useful cooking ingredient, tenderises meat, is light and naturally sweet
milk	poaches fish and vegetables softly, while imparting sweetness
soy sauce	varies hugely according to the brand, ranging from slightly salty to ridiculously so; always taste before you add to a dish if the brand is unfamiliar, and stick to light as dark can often be syrupy

(cont. overleaf)

Nuts & seeds

	All benefit from being toasted in a dry saucepan before being crushed and used as a garnish to provide protein, crunch and glamour. When ground and added to soup, they serve as a gluten- and dairy-free thickener. Some good nuts: cashews, hazelnuts, macadamia nuts, peanuts, pumpkin seeds, pine nuts, walnuts.

Oils

coconut	is having a moment, and therefore being used by some ubiquitously; I like to use it as a base oil in curried and other Asian soups as its flavour carries through
groundnut	a flavourless medium, good for when the flavours from butter or olive oil are unwelcome
olive	a stalwart, reliable for sweating onions and their accompaniments early on; a drizzle of the expensive stuff is a fine way to finish
sesame	use sparingly as a flavour enhancer at the end of cooking

Salt

	Soup needs it. Common kitchen wisdom suggests that liquid tastes best when there's a tsp of salt per quart (an American unit of measure that stands for a quarter of a gallon). Without wanting to get too technical, this amounts to around a ¼ tsp per bowl of soup. It's more than a pinch. Having said that, it is possible to over-salt. See problem-solving.

Spices

chillies	fresh, dried, in flakes or whole, used to impart gentle heat or quite a kick; also indispensable as garnish material
fennel seeds	assist with digestion and inject food with a sweet aniseed flavour
ginger	an anti-inflammatory, fiery when raw, which mellows into something warmer and sweeter when cooked
lemongrass	a powerfully flavoured stalk that adds fragrance
paprika	a clay-red powder that brings a distinct sweetness to soups while imparting colour

Spices (cont.)

pepper	all types are good for sprinkling but black possesses an intense spice and brings out other flavours; white has a more temperate heat that's great for broths; szechuan is not actually a peppercorn, but a dried berry that produces a numbing tingly sensation on your tongue; pink, likewise, is a dried berry, slightly peppery but mostly just fragrant and pretty
turmeric	a faintly bitter spice with powerful medicinal properties, an anti-inflamatory antioxidant that turns everything it touches a vibrant yellow; it is especially attractive in broths and useful for brightening tomato soups

Vegetables

carrots	a member of the holy trinity that is mirepoix – chopped onion, celery and carrot sautéed in fat to form the base of many soups – an essential ingredient in stock making; carrots contain beta-carotene, the antioxidant, which is very good for your immune system, and as a preventer of all sorts of general malaise
celery	another member of mirepoix and another essential for stock making; soups would be duller without its punchy, salty flavour; refreshing when raw.
onions	are the backbone of a great many delicious soups, whether added to the stock pot or sweated slowly to coax out their unparalleled buttery depth; however, sometimes you just can't be bothered to chop an onion – it's not worth the tears; if you're in that sort of mood, here are a couple of soups that manage without: mighty mung (p94), belly broth (p64).
garlic	indispensable smashed in stocks or added to onions and sweated
tomatoes	rich in lycopene, an antioxidant, great for adding sweet acidity

(cont. overleaf)

Vinegars

	Offer tartness to enliven flavour either during or at the end of cooking. I use vinegars a lot. More often than not they can be used interchangeably, but there are some ingredients that certain vinegars pair well with:
balsamic	garlic
cider	apples
red wine	tomatoes
sherry	tomatoes, red peppers, fennel
rice	ginger, pork
white wine	green vegetables

Wine

	Wine added to soup plays a similar role to vinegar but with less acidity and more complexity. Use as much as you like but ideally before you add any other liquid so the alcohol has a chance to burn off. Fortified wines like Madeira and sherry impart a slightly sweet, nutty flavour; Chinese rice wine does something similar. Red wine makes a soup rich, while white wine adds zesty fruitiness.

Other flavourings that don't neatly fit into the categories above

dried mushrooms	when softened in water the liquid is imbued with a welcome savoury flavour, rich with umami, the fifth flavour
honey	I use a lot of it, in part because I'm a beekeeper and surrounded by several squeezy bear containers full of my own, but also because it's easy to dissolve in liquids and you need less of it to get the sweetness you would from sugar.
miso	fermented soybean paste, sweet, savoury and powerfully flavoured; a spoonful of it is a useful flavour enhancer when you've made a soup with water instead of stock
shrimp paste	gives a salty depth and complexity to Asian spice mixes that really works with soup; but it stinks – make sure you're in a well-ventilated space before you fry a mix that contains it

Sometimes we need to eat quickly, and certain ingredients oblige. These soups are packed with vegetables that sing after the briefest dip in stock, providing delicious and nutritious bowls of goodness.

quick

raw

slow

broth

hearty

soup

Instant beetroot & pear with crumbled feta

Thanks to the ready availability of precooked beetroot we've been freed from indelibly stained hands and hours of skewering rock-hard vegetables in order to make this delicious winter warmer. Often accused of being too watery for salads, precooked beetroot finds a happy home in soup where that extra liquid is put to good use. As well as being delicious, beetroot has the benefit of being very nutritious. Ripe pears are essential in this recipe.

Quick stock suggestion:
600ml water, onion, celery,
    bay, thyme, garlic (see p13)

1 tbsp olive oil
1 small onion, finely diced
1 celery stick, finely diced
1 sprig thyme, leaves only
1 garlic clove, chopped
350g cooked beetroot
2 small ripe pears (approx 250g)
300ml vegetable stock

To serve
40g feta
40g walnuts

Heat the oil in a saucepan and add the onion, celery and thyme leaves. Allow the veg to sweat on a low heat for 10 minutes while you grate the beetroot and pear.

When the onions and celery are very soft add the garlic and cook for a further 2 minutes before adding the beetroot and pear. Stir thoroughly, then add the stock and bring to the boil. As soon as this happens, blend and season.

Serve with crumbled feta, crushed walnuts and extra thyme leaves.

Red lentil with braised baby gem & chorizo crumbs

Red lentils are one of the better-behaved pulses. They collapse into silky submission in no time at all, so they're excellent for instant yet hearty gratification. Sadly they lose their raw red hue as they cook, but you can compensate for this by drizzling fried chorizo oil over them. If you want to make this soup meat-free, replace the chorizo with paprika oil (see page 126, sweet potato and ginger soup).

Quick stock suggestion:
1 litre water, onion, celery, carrot, bay, rosemary, lemon peel, Parmesan rind (see p13)

1 tbsp olive oil
1 onion, finely diced
1 celery stick, finely diced
1 carrot, finely diced
100g red lentils
500ml water/stock
1 bushy sprig rosemary, leaves only, finely chopped
1 bay leaf
30g Parmesan, grated (optional)
zest of half a lemon, and juice to taste
1 tsp Dijon mustard
1 raw chorizo sausage (approx 60g), finely cubed
2 baby gems, sliced in half or in wedges

Heat the olive oil over a medium heat. Add the onion, celery and carrot and sweat until the onions are soft and translucent, which should take about 10 minutes. Add the lentils, water or stock, chopped rosemary and bay leaf. Bring to the boil, turn the heat down low, cover and let simmer until the lentils begin to fall apart, which should take about 20 minutes. Stir in the grated Parmesan as well as salt and pepper to taste.

In a small bowl mix the lemon zest with a squeeze of lemon, the Dijon mustard and some black pepper. Have this ready beside your saucepan. Heat a large frying pan over a high heat. When it's very hot, add the diced chorizo and cook until it releases bright red oil and goes crispy. Remove the chorizo, plus a little of the oil from the pan (this is to drizzle over the finished soup). Add the baby gem, cut side down, to the rest of the chorizo oil in the pan, and let it take on a little colour. As soon as this happens tip in the lemon mustard mix and quickly turn the baby gem in the sauce before it evaporates. You may need to add a splash of water. Transfer the braised baby gem to a plate while you ladle your soup into two bowls (this will stop it cooking if you'd like your leaves to retain some crunch).

Top the soups with braised baby gem, chorizo crumbs and any extra oil.

Creamy cabbage & coconut

Cabbage soup is synonymous with an 80s diet that involved drinking bucketfuls of bland liquid in which soft cabbage was suspended, and subsequently feeling miserable (while giving Brassicaceae a bad name). Cook cabbage for too long and it runs the risk of becoming malodorous, but given a relatively quick dip in a pool of richly flavoured coconut milk, as it is here, it's quite delicious.

Quick stock suggestion:
600ml water, onion, celery, bay, garlic, lemon peel (see p13)

200g cabbage (leafier cabbages are best: Savoy, spring greens, cavalo nero, etc)
1 tbsp groundnut oil/ coconut oil
1 small onion, finely chopped
1 garlic clove, chopped
½ tsp dried chilli flakes (less if very hot)
400ml can coconut milk
300ml stock/water
squeeze of lime
coconut chunks, thinly shaved or ready-bought coconut flakes

Prepare your greens by removing the heart or any tough stalks and shred the remaining leaves as finely as you can. You want 200g as your end weight.

Heat the oil in a saucepan and sweat the onion gently for 10 minutes, or until soft and translucent. Add the garlic and chilli flakes and cook for a further minute, then add the shredded cabbage and stir so it gets a good coating of the onion and oil mix. Add the coconut milk and stock and cook over a high heat for about 10 minutes until the cabbage is softened and the liquid has slightly reduced. Season well.

To toast your coconut flakes, move them around a dry frying pan over a high heat for a minute or so, until they brown at the edges. Put them aside until you're ready to serve. Either blend the soup, or serve as it is, topped with a handful of toasted coconut flakes.

Caramelised fennel & butter bean

A soup for fennel lovers, which is a camp I firmly belong to. This recipe gets the best out of the bulb – its nuttiness when slowly sweated with onions as a base, and its toffeeish aniseed flavours when whacked in the oven on high. If it matters to you, fennel – the bulb and seeds – are often cited as galactogogues, which is to say a food that promotes the production of breast milk.

Quick stock suggestion:
1 litre water, onion, celery, bay, garlic, tarragon (see p13)

1 large fennel bulb, or two small (approx 500g)
2 tbsp olive oil, plus extra to drizzle
1 tbsp sherry vinegar
pinch chilli flakes, or more depending on heat
1 tsp fennel seeds, plus a pinch
1 small onion, diced
60ml sherry (manzanilla)
400g can butter beans, drained
500ml stock

Preheat your oven to its highest setting – somewhere around 230°C/210°C fan.

First prepare the fennel. Remove the leafy fronds and put them aside for garnishing. Halve the bulb. Finely chop one half and set aside, then chop the rest into fat matchstick-sized pieces. Toss the matchsticked fennel in a large bowl with half the olive oil, the sherry vinegar, a couple of pinches of chilli flakes, the fennel seeds and a good pinch of salt and pepper. Once the oven is hot, transfer this mixture to a lined baking tray and cook for about 20 minutes – the fennel should be caramelised with blackened tips but will still have a little bite.

Meanwhile, heat the remaining oil in a saucepan and sweat the finely chopped fennel with the onion and an extra pinch of both fennel seeds and chilli flakes for 10 minutes, then add the sherry and boil on high before adding the drained butter beans and stock. Bring everything up to the boil, then reduce to a simmer and cook for another 10 minutes. Blend and check the seasoning.

Serve the butter bean soup with the caramelised fennel on top, plus a few extra fennel seeds, chilli flakes and a drizzle of olive oil.

Celeriac, apple & sage

Celeriac's versatility always surprises me. When cooked it's smooth and velvety, but raw it's delicately crisp and nutty – it veers from being a sophisticated, complex mashed potato replacement to something you might serve as a salad inside a baked potato for light relief. I'm never quite sure which method of preparation is best, but this recipe pays homage to both to get the most out of an earthy and aromatic ingredient.

Quick stock suggestion:
1.5 litres water, onion, celery, carrot, bay, thyme, garlic (see p13)

½ tbsp olive oil
½ tbsp butter
1 onion, finely chopped
½ celery stick, finely chopped
1 tart green apple (Granny Smith or Braeburn are ideal), peeled and finely chopped
handful sage (approx 4 large leaves), shredded
1 garlic clove, chopped
1 tsp cider vinegar
1 tsp honey
350g celeriac, grated
800ml stock

Celeriac and apple topping
1 tart green apple, sliced
½ celery stick, thinly sliced, plus celery leaves
50g celeriac, matchsticked
1 sage leaf, finely shredded
handful flat leaf parsley, roughly chopped
handful walnuts
½ tsp olive oil
½ tsp cider vinegar
½ tsp honey, to taste

Heat the oil in a saucepan and sweat the onion, celery, apple and sage over a very low heat until soft, about 10 minutes. Add the garlic, cider vinegar and honey and cook for a further 2 minutes. Add the celeriac and stock, bring to the boil, then simmer for 25-30 minutes, or until the celeriac is cooked through. Blend until very smooth and check the seasoning.

To prepare the topping, mix everything in a bowl and adjust the seasoning to taste. Serve this smooth soup with a generous scoop of raw salad on top.

Finnish Summer soup

When a friend of mine told me about this recipe, known as *kesakeitto*, I wasn't entirely convinced. Suffice to say that I felt very differently after I'd tried it. Its milky sweetness is heavily reliant on the sweetest of summer's new veg, so make sure you opt for Chantenay carrots or any other baby varieties if they're available. Allspice berries, despite being a widely available supermarket ingredient, are underused, in my opinion, being largely confined to Christmas cakes and stuffing; this recipe takes them out of context and lets them shine. This soup is best eaten on the day it's made.

150g baby potatoes, halved or quartered (depending on size)
10 allspice berries
500ml water
150g baby carrots (sweetest variety possible)
150g cauliflower florets
400ml milk
100g cream cheese/Primula
2 tbsp flour
100g mange tout and peas, mixed
1 tsp honey/sugar
large handful dill, hard stalks removed and roughly chopped
edible flowers, to serve

Place the potatoes and 8 of the allspice berries in a pan with 500ml water and bring to the boil. After 5 minutes, or when the potatoes have started to soften, add the carrots and cauliflower.

In a separate pan gently heat the milk and cream cheese, but do not allow it to boil. Make a slurry by adding a splash of water to the flour in a small bowl and stirring until it dissolves. Pour this mix into the milk while whisking and continue to cook until it thickens. Season with salt and pepper and honey or sugar.

Add the milk mix to the potatoes, carrots and cauliflower along with the mange tout and peas. Add plenty of dill – the more the better – and divide between bowls. Crush the remaining allspice berries with the back of a knife and sprinkle them on top to taste, then sprinkle with edible flowers (I get mine online from maddocksfarmorganics.co.uk).

Maple cauliflower with chicory & hazelnuts

A generous pile of bitter leaves is a welcome foil to the caramelised cauliflower in this recipe and has the added benefit of making your soup look rather dramatic. If anything is going to convert a cauliflower hater, it's this velvety concoction.

Quick stock suggestion:
800ml water, onion, celery, carrot, garlic, bay, parsley stalks (see p13)

600g cauliflower florets
1 tbsp maple syrup
1 tbsp olive oil
1 onion, finely chopped
1 garlic clove, chopped
400ml vegetable stock

To serve
1 red chicory
handful flat leaf parsley
dash red wine vinegar
dash olive oil
40g hazelnuts, dry roasted in a
   pan and smashed with the
   back of a knife

Preheat the oven to 220°C/200°C fan and line a large tray with baking paper. Break up the cauliflower until you have very small florets. Cut up any large stalks – you want to make sure that everything cooks evenly. Mix the maple syrup and ½ tbsp olive oil in the bottom of a large bowl, then add the cauliflower and toss until covered. Season well with salt and black pepper and tip into the prepared baking tray (or two trays if necessary, as you want the cauliflower to be well spread out). Roast in the oven for 20-25 minutes, or until the edges are blackened and the stalks have softened.

While the cauliflower is in the oven, heat the rest of the oil in a saucepan and sweat the onion over a very low heat until soft and translucent. Add the garlic and cook for a further 2 minutes before adding the stock. Tip in most of the cooked cauliflower, reserving 2 heaped tbsps for garnishing. Pour everything into a blender and blitz until very smooth, then season with salt and pepper and return it to the pan. Cook a little longer if you'd like it thicker, or let it down with water if you'd prefer it thinner.

To serve, finely shred the red chicory and chop the parsley, then mix them together with the red wine vinegar and olive oil. Season well and pile onto the soup along with the extra maple-roasted florets and the smashed hazelnuts.

Nutty parsnip & lemon

For the parsnip crisps

1 parsnip (approx 100g),
   ribboned using a peeler,
   discard core if very tough)
1 tsp olive oil
zest of half a lemon, plus
squeeze of juice

For the soup

1 tbsp olive oil
1 onion, chopped
1 stick celery, chopped
1 bay leaf
1 twig thyme
1 garlic clove, chopped
4 parsnips (approx 400g),
   grated or mandolined,
   discard cores if very tough)
600ml almond milk
1 tsp honey
1 tbsp ground almonds
1-3 tsp lemon juice

To serve

Zest of half a lemon
1 tbsp flaked almonds, toasted
Fruity olive oil, to drizzle

Poaching parsnips in milk brings out their sweetness and makes them really nutty. Poaching them in almond milk, even more so – though any milk will work for this soup, which is rich and creamy and would also work beautifully as a starter.

Preheat the oven to 150°C/130°C fan. Prepare the parsnip crisps by tossing the strips in olive oil, lemon zest, a squeeze of lemon juice and plenty of salt and pepper. Spread them out on a tray (or two trays, depending on size – it's important that the parsnip is spread out) lined with baking paper, and roast them in the oven for about 20 minutes, until golden and crispy.

In the meantime heat the oil in a saucepan and sweat the onion, celery and herbs over a very low heat until soft, about 10 minutes. Add the garlic and cook for a further 2 minutes before adding the grated parsnip. Stir well and add the milk. Bring to the boil, then immediately reduce the heat and simmer for about 20-25 minutes, or until the parsnips are cooked through and have no bite.

Blend, add the ground almonds, honey and lemon juice, then blend again and adjust the seasoning (you may want a little more lemon juice). Serve with parsnip crisps, flaked almonds, lemon zest and a drizzle of fruity olive oil.

Classic pea with pumpkin seed crunch

A crowd-pleasing vegetable if ever there was one, peas have been used to wean babies since the 14th century. There's even mention of them in Chaucer's *Canterbury Tales*. And in frozen form they've been feeding the masses regardless of the season since 1950. Toasted pumpkin seeds add welcome crunch to this soup, while also sneaking in some extra nutrients. Roughly torn strips of prosciutto are also a lovely addition.

Quick stock suggestion:
800ml water, onion, celery, carrot, lemon peel, bay, pea pods (see p13)

For the soup
1 tbsp olive oil
1 small onion, finely chopped
80ml white wine
400ml vegetable stock
500g frozen peas
1 tsp lemon juice

For the topping
30g pumpkin seeds
handful mint, finely shredded
30g pecorino, grated
zest of half a lemon, plus 1 tsp lemon juice
½ garlic clove, finely grated
½ tbsp olive oil
1 tbsp capers, rinsed and roughly chopped
50g proscuitto, shredded (optional)

Heat the oil in a saucepan and add the onion. Sweat it for 10 minutes over a very low heat. Turn the heat to high and add the wine, letting it bubble away for several minutes. Add the stock and peas, bring to the boil, then simmer for 2 minutes before blending, seasoning and adding the lemon juice.

To make the topping, start by toasting the pumpkin seeds in a dry frying pan over a medium heat until they pop and turn brown. Roughly chop the seeds and put them in a bowl with the rest of the ingredients and salt and pepper. Serve the soup with generous spoonfuls of the seed mix on top.

Posh baked bean (roast red pepper & white bean)

This is my go-to store cupboard dinner. You could use any white bean but it makes sense to use haricot, of baked bean fame – because there's something pleasingly Heinz about this recipe.

For the soup
1 tbsp olive oil
3cm piece cured chorizo, finely diced (optional)
1 onion, finely chopped
2 garlic cloves, finely sliced
1 tbsp tomato purée
120ml red wine
400g can chopped tomatoes
400g can haricot beans, drained
200g roast red peppers from a jar (drained weight), finely sliced, plus 1 tbsp brine

For the yoghurt blob
2 tbsp soft goat's cheese
2 tbsp natural yoghurt
1 tbsp grated Parmesan
1 tsp lemon juice (optional)

To serve
handful parsley, torn
10 pitted black olives, chopped

Heat the oil in a saucepan and add the chorizo if using. Fry it for a minute, then turn down the temperature and add the onion. Allow it to sweat for 10 minutes until it's translucent and very soft. Stir in the garlic and cook for 2 minutes, then add the tomato purée and cook for another 2 minutes. Turn the heat up and add the red wine, let it reduce by half, then add the chopped tomatoes, the haricot beans, red peppers and brine, along with a can of water.

Bring back to the boil and simmer for 10 minutes, or until the flavours have come together. Season with salt and pepper.

In a small bowl mix the goat's cheese, yoghurt and Parmesan. Season well and taste. You may need to add a little lemon juice, but if your yoghurt and goat's cheese are acidic enough it won't be necessary.

Serve the soup with a generous blob of the yoghurt mixture, a handful of parsley and some black olives.

Salmon, edamame & wasabi

600ml fish stock (see p13)
2 tsp fish sauce
2 tsp soy sauce
1 tsp honey
1 tsp white miso paste
150g udon noodles, to serve
200g frozen edamame beans
1½ tsp wasabi paste
2 salmon fillets, thinly sliced
1 tsp sesame seeds, toasted till
    coloured in a dry frying pan

A soup that takes 10 minutes to make and will satisfy a sushi craving at a fraction of the cost and with considerably less effort. The combination of soft udon noodles and silky salmon with the bite of wasabi-spiced broth is instantly satiating.

Place the stock, fish sauce, soy sauce, honey and miso paste in a saucepan, whisk to combine and bring to the boil. Reduce the heat and simmer gently for 10 minutes.

Cook the udon noodles according to the packet instructions, drain and rinse them thoroughly under cold water. Divide the noodles between two bowls.

Add the edamame to the soup and cook for 2 minutes before adding the wasabi. Taste and add an extra ½ tsp if you would like more heat. Pour the hot liquid on top of the noodles straightaway, then add the sliced salmon just before serving so that it's still a little raw. Sprinkle with toasted sesame seeds and serve with a little extra wasabi on the side for the brave.

Sweetcorn with lemongrass, crab & lime

This recipe falls somewhere between a milky sweetcorn chowder and an aromatic Asian broth, having the texture of the former and the piquancy of the latter.

1 tbsp groundnut oil
1 onion, finely chopped
1 garlic clove
½ red bird's eye chilli, seeds removed and finely sliced (reserve other half for topping)
2 lemongrass stalks, finely sliced
200g sweetcorn (frozen is fine)
1 yellow or orange pepper
500ml milk

For the topping
150g white crab meat
zest of 1 lime, juice to taste
½ red bird's eye chilli, finely sliced
1 tsp olive oil
handful coriander, chopped
handful chives, or 1 small spring onion, chopped

Heat the oil in a saucepan and gently cook the onion for 10 minutes, or until it's soft and translucent. Add the garlic, chilli and lemongrass and cook for 2 minutes more before adding the sweetcorn and pepper. Stir to heat through for a couple of minutes, then add the milk and bring to the boil. Immediately reduce to a simmer and cook for 20 minutes. Blitz the soup and adjust the seasoning, adding a little milk to loosen to your desired consistency.

Mix all the ingredients for the crab salad, season with salt and pepper and serve on top.

Chinese beef & tofu

This soup originated in the Zhejiang province of eastern China and this recipe is taken from the brilliant *The Dumpling Sisters* cookbook, which I was lucky enough to work on with authors Amy and Julie Zhang.

Texturally it's a slightly unusual soup. Thickened with cornflour, it has a certain gloopiness that might not be to everyone's taste; however, I would urge you to embrace it as a fine example of *waat*, one of the most sought-after mouthfeels in Chinese cooking. This name is given to foods that are silky, slippery and smooth.

Despite being easy to make and not requiring a stock, this soup packs a fragrant, flavoursome punch.

4 dried shitake mushrooms
150g beef mince
1 tsp + 1½ tbsp cornflour
700ml water
2 tsp light soy sauce
¼ tsp fine salt
¼ tsp ground white pepper, more to taste
1 egg white
1 small bunch coriander, leaves torn
handful baby leaf spinach
80g soft tofu, chopped into cubes

Pour 100ml hot water over the mushrooms and leave them to soften for 30 minutes; then drain and finely slice them, reserving the liquid. Combine the beef with 1 tsp cornflour and set aside.

Bring 700ml water and the reserved 100ml mushroom water to the boil in a large saucepan, and add the soy, salt and pepper, mushrooms and beef – crumbling the latter to break up any lumps. Reduce and simmer for 10 minutes.

Dissolve the remaining 1½ tbsp of cornflour in 50ml water. Turn the temperature up a bit and add the cornflour slurry to the pan, continuing to stir until the soup thickens.

Drizzle in the beaten egg white, whisking continuously, then stir in the coriander and spinach and cook until both have just wilted. Finally, add the tofu to heat through just before serving.

These soups are unconventional. They are not only served cold but also involve no cooking during assembly, meaning they're brimming with unadulterated nutrients. Raw recipes rely upon a solid starting point so arm yourself with the season's finest produce and ready your blender.

quick

raw

slow

broth

hearty

soup

Cooling cucumber with aromatic lemon salsa

The salsa in this recipe is a game-changer: put it on anything and everything – salads, pasta, egg-based brunches. Just be aware that nothing on the plate will get noticed as much as the salsa.

For the preserved lemon salsa
20g parsley leaves
20g coriander leaves
20g pitted green olives
50g preserved lemons, pips removed
6 tbsp water
2 tbsp olive oil

For the soup
100g natural yoghurt
1 large cucumber (300g)
handful baby leaf spinach
2 tsp preserved lemon brine from jar

Place all the preserved lemon salsa ingredients up to the water in a blender and blitz. Add the oil and blend until just incorporated.

Clean out the blender and blend the yoghurt, cucumber, spinach and brine. Season and pour into two bowls before adding a generous topping of the preserved lemon mix.

Gazpacho with wilted basil

Perhaps the best known salad soup, gazpacho hails from Andalusia in Spain. I find that Romano peppers – the long red ones with darker skin – tend to be better than standard bell peppers for this recipe as they are sweeter and have a more tender skin. Because of the raw garlic element, this recipe is best if made and then left for about 30 minutes to let the flavours develop before it is eaten.

For the soup
2-4 ripe vine tomatoes (approx 400g)
1 small avocado
2 red Romano peppers, half of 1 reserved for the topping
2 spring onions
1 small garlic clove, microplaned
½ cucumber, peeled (200g)
1 tsp sherry vinegar
1 tsp lemon juice
zest of half a lemon
1 tsp honey (unnecessary if your tomatoes are very sweet)
¼ tsp hot paprika

To serve
handful basil leaves
1 tbsp good olive oil
½ red Romano pepper, diced

Place everything in a blender with plenty of salt and pepper – note that cold food requires more seasoning. Blend, then adjust the seasoning according to the sweetness of your ingredients – you may need a little extra honey and sherry vinegar if your tomatoes aren't as ripe as they could be.

Place the basil leaves in a sieve over the sink and pour boiling water over them to wilt them. Immediately run cold water over them to stop them turning black. Gently squeeze them to remove excess moisture then place them in a bowl with the olive oil, plenty of sea salt and some diced red Romano pepper. Spoon this on top of each bowl before serving.

Mango, avocado & lime

Avocados have a talent for making everything they're whizzed up with turn to velvet, but they also carry the risk of making things a little too rich. Lime comes to the rescue in this delicious mix. Use just the first three ingredients if you'd like to make a smoothie rather than a soup.

2 large avocados (400g flesh)
2 large mangos (600g flesh)
6 tbsp lime juice (from 2-4 limes) plus zest to serve
2 jalapeño peppers, a little reserved for the garnish
2 spring onions
½ small garlic clove or pinch garlic powder

Blend everything and adjust the seasoning to taste. Add water to obtain desired consistency. Top with lime zest and some chopped jalapeño pepper.

Spiced kale with cashew cream & kale crisps

Nutritionally dense and seriously cheap, kale has reached celebrity status in the last couple of years for good reason. If the idea of eating it raw frightens you, know that you are not alone. My only advice is to arm yourself with a powerful blender and all those fibrous stalks and stems will be turned to silk.

50g cashews
50g desiccated coconut
200g kale (destalked weight 150g)
1 tbsp lemon juice
½ tsp paprika
½ tbsp olive oil
1 tsp ground cumin
1 tsp ground coriander
pinch turmeric
½ avocado
2 tsp honey
500ml water

Preheat the oven to 80°C/60°C fan, or whatever your lowest setting is. Place the cashews and the coconut in two separate glasses and cover both with hot water. Allow them to soak and soften for 20 minutes. Rip the stalks off the kale and break the leaves into smallish pieces, about 5cm in length at most. Place half in a bowl to make kale crisps, and keep the other half to blend for the soup.

To make the cashew cream, discard the liquid from the soaked nuts and place them in the blender with the lemon juice, a pinch of salt and about 100ml water. Blend to a paste. Take 1 tbsp of this cashew cream and add to the kale reserved for making crisps, along with the olive oil. Massage everything into the leaves then tip them onto a lined oven tray, ensuring they are spread out. Season with the paprika and a bit of sea salt and place in the oven for 30-40 minutes. The kale is ready when it has dried out and become brittle and crispy.

Scoop the remaining cashew cream out of the blender and reserve. Without bothering to clean the blender, tip the remaining kale in, along with the coconut and its liquid and the rest of the ingredients. Blend until smooth, adding a little extra liquid to obtain desired consistency. Adjust the seasoning, divide into bowls and serve with a swirl of cashew cream and a pile of kale crisps.

Sunshine soup

Yellow food is packed full of cartenoids, which are great antioxidants, good for your immune system and general protection against harmful bacteria. This sunny-coloured soup will provide a fair few of these. Obviously the sort of corn that is freshly picked and comes cloaked in its own leafy shield is best, but don't bother buying fresh if it's out of season – frozen corn is a fine alternative. All nuts can be used to thicken soup, after they've been softened by soaking, but cashews are the hands-down winners.

40g cashews
2 corn cobs, kernels removed, or 200g frozen corn
2 yellow peppers
½ garlic clove or pinch garlic powder
1 spring onion
200ml water

To serve
1 spring onion, shredded
pinch chilli flakes

Soak the cashews in warm water for about half an hour. Drain them and put them in a blender with the rest of the ingredients. Blend everything, gradually adding the water till you reach your desired consistency. Season with salt and pepper and top with finely shredded spring onion and chilli flakes.

Time allows several things to happen: for slow-cooked meat to dissolve, for stubborn pulses to yield, for familiar ingredients to blend and mingle and take on unexpected new hues. Great flavours come to those who wait.

quick

raw

slow

broth

hearty

soup

Belly
Broth

This broth might take several hours to make, but you'll be active for none of them and your home will smell of sweet spices for the duration. The star ingredient is Shaoxing rice wine, a Chinese cooking wine made from fermented glutinous rice. With a flavour that can be likened to a dry fruity sherry, it lends a deeply savoury note to dishes.

For the broth
200g skinless pork belly,
  sliced into 2cm pieces
1.5 litres water
50ml light soy sauce
50ml Chinese Shaoxing rice
  wine
4cm root ginger, sliced
  into matchsticks
3 garlic cloves, thinly sliced
1 star anise
1 bird's eye chilli, sliced
  lengthways
pinch ground white pepper,
  or 3 white peppercorns
1 small bunch coriander,
  stalks only, tied up with
  string (leaves reserved for
  garnishing)

**For the sticky pork
(optional)**
1 tbsp light soy sauce
1 tbsp honey

To serve
200g rice vermicelli
4 small pak choi, halved or
  quartered lengthways
1 spring onion, finely sliced
handful coriander leaves

Place the pork belly in a saucepan, cover it with cold water and bring to the boil, skimming the water as scum appears. Drain and rinse the meat and saucepan, then return the meat to the pan with all of the broth ingredients. Bring to a boil, then reduce to a gentle simmer and cook, uncovered, for 2 hours.

Check if the meat is tender, and give it a little longer if necessary. Now you have the option to make your pork sticky (as pictured); if you don't want to do this, skip to the following stage.

Remove the pork from the broth and dry it with paper towel. Mix the honey and soy sauce in a small bowl and place it beside the hob, alongside another bowl or vessel for collecting excess fat, and a plate for the pork. When you have everything ready, heat a frying pan until very hot. Fry the pork for 1 minute on each side until it releases its fat and starts to blacken. Remove the pork to the plate with a slotted spoon and drain the fat. Return the pork to the hot pan with the soy and honey mix and stir around to coat. As soon as the pork pieces are coated and sticky transfer them to the plate.

Remove the coriander stalks from the broth and discard them, then add the rice vermicelli and pak choi to the liquid and cook for an additional 3-4 minutes, or until the greens are wilted and the noodles tender. Serve with the pork, sliced spring onion and coriander leaves.

Cuban black bean & ham hock

This recipe calls for ham hock stock – a recipe for which can be found on page 13. If you don't have time to make it use a good chicken stock. Better still, I can highly recommend quadrupling these quantities, in which case you can simply pop a ham hock directly in the saucepan with the rest of the ingredients. Do make sure you've soaked your ham hock in plenty of cold water first to reduce the saltiness.

Ordinarily I can take or leave green peppers, but I feel they do something wonderful when slow-cooked like this. The winning ingredient is cider vinegar, a teaspoon of which manages to unify and enliven everything in the pot. You'll have to try it to see what I mean.

100g black beans (soaked in cold water overnight)
1 small onion, chopped
1 green pepper, chopped
2 garlic cloves, chopped
1 litre liquid (500ml ham hock stock & 500ml water, or chicken stock)
1 tbsp olive oil
1 tsp cider vinegar
100g ham hock, shredded
2 tbsp natural yoghurt
handful coriander leaves, to serve

Place the soaked and drained black beans in a saucepan with the onion, green pepper, garlic, liquid and olive oil. Bring to the boil and simmer very gently for 3 hours, with the lid partially covering the saucepan. Occasionally check the pot, adding a little more liquid is necessary. After 3 hours check to see whether the beans are soft. If they are add the vinegar and cook for a further 5 minutes. Then check the seasoning and serve with shredded ham hock, a blob of yoghurt and lots of chopped coriander.

Hungarian goulash

The paprika produced in Hungary has a certain luminosity to it when viewed next to the more commonly available stuff from Spain, Peru or China. In these regions the sun turns the paprika a dark red, whereas the cooler climate in Hungary allows it to stay a bright brick colour, giving it a vibrancy that gleefully makes it through to the final dish. Although a hot variety is available, sweet Hungarian paprika is more common and is what I have used here. It's worth investing in some. You'll certainly get through it quickly if you develop a liking for this recipe.

200g beef shin, or other stewing beef, diced into 2cm pieces
1 tsp caraway seeds
1 tbsp oil
1 small onion, finely chopped
2 garlic cloves, chopped
2 sprigs thyme, leaves only
1 tbsp sweet Hungarian paprika
1 bay leaf
1 tbsp tomato purée
1 tsp red wine vinegar
1 green pepper, chopped into 1cm pieces
1 waxy potato (approx 120g), diced into 2cm pieces
800ml beef stock

To serve
2 tbsp sour cream
1 tbsp chives, chopped

Preheat the oven to 170°C/150°C fan. Add the caraway and a couple of pinches of sea salt to the beef, massaging it in. Put the oil in an overproof pan or casserole dish over a high heat. Brown the beef, in two batches if necessary, for 5 minutes – you'll get a far better result if you resist the temptation to move the meat around the pan. Browning one side of the meat is sufficient. Remove with a slotted spoon and set aside. Add the onion, garlic, thyme, paprika and bay to the pan and cook over a low heat for 10 minutes, or until the onions have softened. Then add the tomato purée and cook for a couple of minutes before adding the vinegar. Return the meat to the pan with the peppers, potato and stock. Bring everything to the boil and transfer to the oven.

After an hour check to see if the meat is meltingly tender. If the goulash is still too liquid for your liking, you can cook it on the hob without a lid for 10 minutes or so until it has reduced. Serve with sour cream and chives.

Hearty dal with cauliflower rice

Good old dal. It would be easy on your bank balance and no bad thing health-wise to eat it every day. This very simple dish is delicious and nourishing. The cauliflower tarka is the party on top.

For the dal

200g yellow split peas, rinsed
1 green bird's eye chilli, seeds removed and finely chopped
3 garlic cloves, sliced
3cm root ginger, sliced in matchsticks
½ tbsp turmeric
¼ tsp fine salt

For the cauliflower rice tarka

½ tbsp coconut oil, or groundnut oil
1 shallot, finely sliced
1 tsp mustard seeds
1 tsp cumin seeds
200g cauliflower florets, pulsed in a blender to resemble rice
1 tsp onion seeds
handful coriander leaves
2 tbsp pomegranate seeds

Cover the rinsed split peas with 1.5 litres water. Bring to the boil, skim, then add the chilli, garlic, ginger and turmeric and simmer for 2 hours. Every 20 minutes or so use a small whisk to beat the lentils into submission, and add a little water if necessary. When you're ready to serve them, add the salt and loosen them with a little boiling water.

When the dal is ready, heat the oil in a large frying pan over a medium to high heat. Fry the shallot until it starts to brown, then add the mustard and cumin seeds and stir until the mustard begin to pop. Toss in the cauliflower and stir for about 1 minute. Turn off the heat and add the onion seeds, coriander, salt and pepper. Heap generously on top of two bowls of dal and finish each off with pomegranate seeds and extra coriander leaves.

Iranian herb & pomegranate with meatballs

Sour, tangy and richly flavoured, this soup owes its punch to pomegranate syrup, added 20 minutes before the end of cooking. Other than that it is comprised mostly of herbs – so it's worth taking a trip to the market to buy bunches with flavoursome stalks that will greatly contribute to your final dish.

1 tbsp oil
1 small onion, diced
2 garlic cloves, diced
¼ tsp turmeric
1 bunch spring onions, roughly chopped (1 onion, finely chopped, to be reserved for the meatballs)
1 litre water
50g yellow split peas, rinsed
200g ground lamb
1 bunch parsley, stalks finely chopped, leaves kept whole
1 bunch coriander, stalks finely chopped, leaves kept whole
1 bunch mint, leaves only
20ml pomegranate molasses (syrup), plus extra to taste

To serve
2 tbsp natural yoghurt
2 tbsp pomegranate seeds

Heat the oil in a saucepan and sweat the onion over a very low heat until soft – about 10 minutes. Add the garlic, turmeric, spring onions and parsley and coriander stalks and cook for a further 2 minutes before adding the water and split peas. Bring to the boil, then simmer for 40 minutes.

To make the meatballs, mix the lamb with a pinch of each herb and the single spring onion, season well and form into walnut-sized balls. You should get about 16. Put them in the fridge until you're ready to cook them.

When the split peas in the soup pot are getting soft, add the meatballs. Roughly chop the remaining herb leaves and add these along with the pomegranate molasses. Bring back to the boil, then reduce to a simmer and cook for a further 20 minutes. Check to see if the meatballs are cooked through, and check the seasoning. Add extra pomegranate molasses, if you think you'd like more tang.

Serve with a dollop of yoghurt and some pomegranate seeds sprinkled on top.

Jacket potato with saffron

Two comfort foods – the soup and the jacket potato – rolled into one. There are faster ways of making a potato soup but all the goodness is in the skin, and for the skin to develop the most deliciously crispy exterior possible it needs time. The flesh within fares well, too, when it is slow-cooked, becoming considerably creamier than it would otherwise.

Quick stock suggestion:
1.5 litres water, carrot, celery, bay, thyme, leek, lemon peel (see p13)

2 baking potatoes
1 tsp olive oil, plus a splash
½ tsp rock salt
30g butter
1 large leek, finely chopped
1 garlic clove, finely chopped
30ml white wine
1 big pinch saffron
700ml chicken or veg stock
juice of half a lemon (approx 1 tbsp), plus more to serve

Preheat the oven to 180°C/160°C fan. Prick the potatoes, rub them with olive oil and sprinkle them with rock salt. Place them directly on an oven shelf and bake them for 2-2½hrs. When they are ready remove them from the oven and allow to cool a little before splitting them, scooping the flesh out and cutting the crispy skins into large triangles to use as croutons or dippers. Set these aside while you make the soup. The potato skin pieces should be incredibly crispy. If they're not, or you're not eating the soup straight away, they can be placed in a hot oven for 5 minutes just before serving.

Melt the butter in a pan with a splash of olive oil, then add the leek and cook over a low heat for 10 minutes, or until very soft. Add the garlic and cook for another 2 minutes. Pour in the wine with the saffron and let the alcohol reduce for a couple of minutes before tipping in the potato flesh to heat through. Add the stock and bring to the boil. Cook for 10 minutes, then blitz in the blender with the lemon juice and plenty of salt and pepper to taste. Serve with the crispy potato skins.

All seasons Christmas soup (carrot, cardamom & orange)

British-grown carrots were mostly a summer vegetable up until the 1990s, but these days, thanks to the British farmers' practice of putting their crop to bed for the winter – keeping them in the ground and covering them with straw – fresh carrots are available all year round. A great contender for a light Christmas soup, this would also be refreshing served chilled on a summer's day – though if you were going to do that I'd swap the leek for an onion, as leeks can make things taste a bit wintery.

Quick stock suggestion:
1.5 litres water, carrot, leek, bay, thyme, orange peel, garlic (see p13)

¼ tsp ground cardamom (see method)
800g carrots, cut into small batons or 1cm rounds
1 tbsp olive oil
2 tsp honey
zest and juice of half an orange
¼ tsp cumin
1 leek, finely sliced
1 garlic clove, finely chopped
700ml vegetable stock

For the topping
2 tbsp natural yoghurt
4 pitted dates, finely chopped
zest and juice of half an orange
1 red bird's eye chilli, seeds removed and finely chopped
handful mint, shredded
½ tsp coriander seeds, crushed with the back of a knife
½ tsp cumin seeds
1 tsp honey

Preheat the oven to 200°C/180°C fan. To prepare the cardamom, crush approximately 10 pods in a pestle and mortar or with the back of a heavy knife. Remove the pods and further crush the seeds. Measure ¼ tsp (you may need to crush more).

Toss the carrots in half the oil, honey, orange juice and zest, cumin and salt and pepper. Spread them out on a large baking tray so that they have plenty of space. Cook them for 40 minutes, by which point they should be tender and blackening at the edges.

Heat the remaining oil in a saucepan and cook the leeks on a low temperature for 10 minutes, then add the garlic and cook for a further 2 minutes. Tip in the cooked carrots and stir to heat through before adding the stock and bringing to the boil. Simmer for 10 minutes, then blend. Add a little water if the soup is too thick. Put a spoonful of yoghurt on each bowl of soup, then mix the remaining ingredients and scatter on top.

Souk soup

I daren't call this harira – though really that's what it is – because I've rather heretically added wine to a soup that's traditionally eaten to break fast during Ramadan. To tell the truth, whenever I've eaten this soup in Morocco I've been struck by how bland it is. My version is reminiscent of the souk: of slow-cooked lamb tagines and vendors pedalling spices everywhere you turn.

200g lamb neck, diced into small bite-sized pieces, about 1.5cm
2 tsp cumin seeds, half ground with a pestle and mortar or blender
1 tbsp olive oil
1 small red onion, finely diced
1 celery stick, finely diced (leaves reserved for garnish)
1 carrot, finely diced
3cm root ginger, sliced into matchsticks
2 garlic cloves, sliced
1 tsp turmeric
1 tsp sweet paprika
1 tsp ground cinnamon
1 tbsp tomato purée
30ml red wine
1 bay leaf
½ can chopped tomatoes (200g)
40g green lentils, rinsed

To serve
handful coriander, parsley and celery leaves
1 lemon, cut into wedges

Preheat your oven to 170°C/150°C fan. Use a piece of paper towel to blot away any excess moisture from the lamb. Season the meat with the cumin and a good couple of pinches of sea salt and put aside.

Put the oil in an ovenproof pan or casserole dish over a high heat. Brown the lamb, in two batches if necessary, for 5 minutes – you'll get a far better result if you resist the temptation to move the meat around the pan. Browning one side of the meat is sufficient. Remove it with a slotted spoon and set aside. Turn down the heat, add the onion, celery, carrot and ginger and sweat them gently for 10 minutes or until everything is very soft. Return the meat to the pan with the garlic, turmeric, paprika and cinnamon and stir before adding the tomato purée. Stir for another minute, then pour in the red wine to deglaze the pan. Next add the bay leaf, chopped tomatoes, 500ml water and the lentils, and bring to the boil. Cover and transfer to the oven for an hour.

Once the lamb is tender, remove the soup from the oven and stir in the chopped coriander and parsley, reserving a little extra to scatter on top with the celery leaves. Season well. Serve with wedges of lemon.

Sticky shallot, sprout & raisin

Onions play the supporting role in a great many soups but this one lets them shine. Although shallots are a little sweeter than common onions, they're also slightly more potent with more notable garlic tones so I think they offer something a bit richer. However, I'm aware that they're more hassle in terms of preparation, so feel free to use normal onions or a mixture of both.

The word soup derives from the Latin suppa, which translates as 'bread soaked in broth'. So this really is a soup, in the original meaning of the word.

1 tbsp olive oil
1 tbsp butter
500g shallots, thinly sliced
    lengthways
1 tsp sugar
1 garlic clove, chopped
30g raisins, a mix of dark and
    golden if possible
60ml Madeira/dry sherry
700ml beef stock (see p13)
100g Brussels sprouts, shaved
    (ideally with a mandoline)
2 slices French bread
30g Gruyère, grated

Place the butter and oil in wide-based non-stick saucepan over a medium low heat. Add the shallots and sugar to the pan, along with some salt and pepper. Cook them very gently for 30-40 minutes, stirring occasionally, until they're caramelised (if you're not using a non-stick pan and things begin to stick just add a splash of water). Add the garlic, cook for a couple of minutes more, then add the raisins and Madeira. Let the alcohol burn off for a couple of minutes, before pouring in the stock. Bring to the boil, then simmer for 20 minutes. Add the sprouts and bring back to the boil, then lower the heat and simmer for a mere minute if you'd like your sprouts to retain some bite, or longer if you'd like them soft. Check the seasoning.

Just before your soup is ready, place the bread on a tray lined with baking paper under a preheated grill. When it's lightly toasted on both sides, add a generous pile of cheese to each piece and place it back under to melt.

Put a piece of Gruyère toast in each bowl and ladle the sticky onion soup on top.

A chapter full of flavoursome liquids that boast texture and interest. These are soups to cleanse, restore and comfort.

quick

raw

slow

broth

hearty

soup

Beef pho

The combination of slippery noodles, tender beef, rich meaty broth and clean, crunchy garnishes makes pho the stuff of cravings. The more crunchy stuff the better, so make sure you serve it as the Vietnamese do, with bowls of extra bits to add as you eat.

200g sirloin or fillet steak, thinly sliced

For the broth
1 cinnamon stick
1 star anise
2 cloves
4 cardamom pods
1 litre beef stock (see p13)
2 tbsp soy sauce
1 bird's eye chilli, split
1 onion, cut into quarters
2 garlic cloves, smashed
2 slices ginger
2 tsp honey

To serve
150g rice noodles
dash groundnut oil
¼ Chinese cabbage, thinly shredded
50g bean sprouts
10 cherry tomatoes, halved
2 radishes, mandolined
1 lime, cut into wedges to squeeze on top
handful each mint, basil, Thai basil, coriander, or whatever is available

Place the steak in the freezer for about 15 minutes. When it is nice and cold, use your sharpest knife to cut the thinnest slices of meat you can manage. Cover the sliced meat with clingfilm and leave it on the side to come back to room temperature – if the meat is still cold when you use it, it will cool the broth.

Place the cinnamon, star anise, cloves and cardamom in a pan and dry roast them over a medium heat for 1-2 minutes, until toasty and fragrant. Scoop the cardamom pods out and crush them with a pestle and mortar or with the back of a heavy knife. Remove the pods and crush the seeds that are left as best you can before returning them to the pan. Now add the beef stock, soy, chilli, onion, garlic, ginger and honey. Bring to the boil, reduce the heat and simmer for 30 minutes.

Meanwhile, get everything ready for serving. Cook the rice noodles, then rinse them well in cold water, mix with a dash of groundnut oil and divide them between the bowls. Top with the cabbage, bean sprouts, tomatoes and radishes followed by the slices of raw beef and the herbs.

Taste the broth, adjust the seasoning, and then strain it (optional). Make sure that when you serve it, it's piping hot so that it cooks the thinly sliced beef almost instantly. Serve with the lime wedges and any extra bits of prepped veg and herbs so that people can personalise their own pho.

Springtime veg patch broth (asparagus & radish)

Use proper English asparagus for this recipe if you can because the tough thick stalks make for a great stock. Edible flowers like nasturtiums and violas are deliciously peppery and go brilliantly with this homage to British spring veg. They are increasingly being sold at greengrocers' in little boxes. Otherwise they're widely available online, and whatever you don't sprinkle on the soup you can toss in with a green salad or use to decorate a cake.

Quick stock suggestion:
1.5 litres water, leek, celery, carrot, parsley stalks, garlic, asparagus ends, broad bean pods, bay (see p13)

800ml vegetable stock
1 leek, finely sliced
4 small turnips, quartered
6 radishes, half quartered and half thinly sliced (using a mandoline if you have one)
40g broad beans (or peas, frozen of both is fine)
250g asparagus, stalky ends snapped off (and used in quick stock), thinly sliced into rounds and lengthways

To serve
30g pecorino, grated
edible flowers (available from maddocksfarmorganics.com)

First make your quick stock, with a selection of finely chopped vegetables and aromatics, including asparagus ends. After 30 minutes of rapid boiling, which should see the liquid reduced by half, use a sieve to strain the liquid into a new saucepan. Add the leek, turnips and quartered radishes to the stock with a pinch of salt and bring to the boil.

Put the broad beans in a pan of boiling water and cook for 5 minutes. Drain them and run them under cold water before popping them out of their skins and setting aside.

Simmer the broth until the turnips are tender, then add the asparagus and thinly sliced radishes, merely blanching them so that they retain their bite, followed by the broad beans. Check the seasoning, adding more salt if necessary. Serve with grated pecorino, black pepper and a sprinkling of edible flowers.

Cleansing chicken, lemon & mint with buckwheat

This soup is a loose interpretation of the Portuguese and Brazilian *canja de galinha*, which is a version of healing chicken soup – every culture has one. While it's usually served with rice, I've opted for buckwheat.

Buckwheat is one of those wonder ingredients, high in dietary fibre and with the power to regulate blood sugar levels and keep cholesterol in check. Also, despite its misleading name, it's actually a seed, so it's gluten-free. It gives an unusual background flavour to this soup while adding a unique texture. If you're not a fan of buckwheat, quinoa would be a similarly highly nutritious and quick-cooking grain to use.

For the soup
1 litre water
1 lemon, peel removed with peeler and finely sliced, juice reserved for serving
1 shallot, finely sliced
¼ tsp salt
¼ tsp white pepper
1 garlic clove, finely sliced
1 tbsp white wine vinegar
1 tsp honey
1 tsp coriander seeds
½ tsp dried oregano
2–4 chicken thighs (depending on size), bone in and skin removed
100g unroasted buckwheat groats

To serve
4 sprigs mint, leaves only, shredded
Juice of a lemon, to be added according to taste

Place everything in a saucepan and bring to the boil. Reduce the heat and simmer until the chicken is poached – approximately 40 minutes. Remove the chicken and shred it. Stir in the mint and half of the lemon juice, then check the seasoning and add more if necessary. Divide the soup between two bowls and top with the shredded chicken.

Make-ahead coconut water chicken

Marinating meat in coconut water has the rather brilliant effect of tenderising it while imparting sweet, nutty flavours. Add a couple of tablespoons of curry paste and the results are far more flavoursome than a dish this easy deserves to be. I've included a recipe for a quick Thai-style paste here – heavy on the lemongrass and ginger – but you could veer off track if you don't have everything to hand. This recipe is just as delicious without noodles, so if you're looking for something carb-free, just use extra chicken.

1 red bird's eye chilli, seeds removed
1 garlic clove
2 spring onions
1 kaffir lime leaf
1 lemongrass stalk
4cm root ginger
small bunch coriander, stalks only (reserve leaves for garnish)
pinch salt
1 litre coconut water
2-4 chicken thighs (depending on size), bone in, skin removed
200g mange tout, green beans and bean sprouts, a mixture of, all sliced if necessary

To serve
100g rice noodles, cooked
coriander leaves, reserved from bunch used in the paste
1 tbsp peanuts
½ red bird's eye chilli, sliced (possibly less, depending on heat)
1 spring onion, thinly sliced

Put the first 8 ingredients into a blender and blitz to form a rough paste. Add the coconut water, then transfer the lot to a large sandwich bag and add the chicken. Leave overnight for the best meat-tenderising results. If you're short of time, a couple of hours will have some effect too.

When you're ready to eat, decant the contents of the bag into a medium-sized saucepan and bring to the boil, skimming off any scum as it appears (it will be impossible to remove everything without also removing other ingredients so don't worry too much). Reduce the heat to a simmer and poach the chicken – this should take about 45 minutes. When the meat is cooked, remove it from the broth and shred it. Add the green beans, mange tout and bean sprouts to the broth to cook, which will only take a minute, then put the chicken back in. Pour the broth over the noodles (if using) then top with the coriander, peanuts, chilli and spring onion.

Clams & fennel

Clam shells enclose their own salty liquor, which makes them a fantastic ingredient in soup. Always buy clams on the day you intend to use them as they're alive and surprisingly easy to kill between making your purchase and cooking dinner – discovering you've killed them all is devastating. They need to breathe, so take them out of the fishmonger's plastic bag, spread them out on a baking tray, lay a damp tea towel over them and put them in the fridge until needed.

Quick stock suggestion:
1 litre water, onion, fennel, celery, bay, garlic, parsley stalks (see p13)

800g fresh clams
1 tbsp olive oil
1 small fennel bulb, finely chopped
1 shallot, finely chopped
3 garlic cloves, thinly sliced
¼ tsp chilli flakes (or less if very hot)
1 tbsp tomato purée
10 cherry tomatoes, halved or quartered
400g can chickpeas, drained
500ml fish or vegetable stock
120ml amontillado sherry

To serve
parsley, finely chopped
pinch chilli flakes
olive oil, to drizzle

Inspect your clams and discard any that don't close when tapped. Clean them by leaving them covered in plenty of cold water for about 20 minutes, then scoop them out either with your hands or a slotted spoon – you don't want to drain them by tipping the bowl because there may be sand in the bottom.

In a wide-based saucepan, heat the oil and fry the fennel for 5 minutes, or until it begins to soften. Add the shallot, garlic, chilli flakes, tomato purée and cherry tomatoes and cook for another 5 minutes. Tip in the chickpeas and stir to heat them thoroughly, then add the fish stock, a pinch of salt (don't over-salt as clams will also contain salt) and bring to the boil.

Pour in the sherry together with the clams and cover the pan. Cook until the clams have completely opened, shaking the pan a couple of times. This should take about 5 minutes. Toss in the parsley, chilli flakes and a drizzle of olive oil.

Mighty mung

Mung beans – also known as moong and green gram – are touted as healing foods in Chinese and Ayurvedic medicine. Combining them with turmeric, ginger, cider, fennel, vinegar, honey – the roll call of life-giving ingredients – is almost enough to persuade you of your own immortality. This soup is thirst-quenching, cleansing and restorative but it's also absolutely delicious. Mung beans don't need soaking and they cook surprisingly quickly; in fact, like most legumes their cooking times seem to vary depending on what batch you get, so I find it safest to cook them in a separate pan, to catch them at the exact stage I want – tender but not floury. Be wary, this change happens in an instant …

1 litre water
¼ tsp turmeric
¼ tsp salt
1 garlic clove, sliced
3cm root ginger, sliced into matchsticks
1 tbsp cider vinegar
1 tsp honey
1 tsp fennel seeds
½ green bird's eye chilli
2–4 chicken thighs (depending on size), bone in and skin removed
200g mung beans, well rinsed in cold water
olive oil

Place everything apart from the mung beans in a saucepan and bring to the boil. Reduce the heat and simmer until the chicken is poached – about 40 minutes. Remove the chicken and shred it.

In a separate pan cover the mung beans with cold water and bring to the boil. Add a glug of oil, a pinch of salt and simmer until the mung beans are tender. This should take anything between 30 and 45 minutes. When they are ready, drain them and add them to the broth. Divide the soup between two bowls and top with shredded chicken.

Green Thai mussels with courgettes

If you don't fancy making your own Thai curry paste you can always use shop-bought. It might not be quite as fragrant or vibrantly green but it does mean you'll have something to eat in 10 minutes. Thai Taste is a nice brand and is widely available in supermarkets; otherwise look for semi-fresh offerings from smaller brands in the fridge section of good health food shops.

Quick stock suggestion:
500ml water, onion, celery, bay, garlic, kaffir, lemongrass

800g fresh mussels

For the curry paste
1 bunch coriander (reserve some leaves for garnish)
2 garlic cloves
1 lemongrass stalk
2cm root ginger
3 spring onions
1 green bird's eye chilli
1 tbsp groundnut oil
½ tsp shrimp paste (optional)
1 kaffir lime leaf
¼ tsp salt

For the soup
400ml can coconut milk
200ml fish or vegetable stock
fish sauce
1 tsp soy sauce
1 tsp honey
1 large courgette, halved lengthways and cut into 1cm crescents

To serve
1 lime, cut into wedges
100g jasmine or sticky rice, cooked
reserved coriander leaves

Scrub the mussels and remove the beards, discarding any that don't open.

Make the curry paste by blitzing everything together in a blender. Depending on your machine you may need to chop things first. Heat a large saucepan over a medium heat and cook the curry paste for a couple of minutes (if you are using shop-bought you may need to add a little oil to your pan first – see what it says on the label).

Add the coconut milk, stock, fish sauce, soy and honey and bring to the boil, then simmer for 15 minutes. Stir in the courgettes and bring back to the boil, then add the mussels. Cover with a lid and cook, shaking occasionally, until the mussels open – this should take about 5 minutes.

Serve with the reserved coriander leaves, wedges of lime, and a bowl of cooked rice on the side. After you've eaten your mussels, spoon the rice into the broth.

Mushroom dashi

A classic, clean soup which utilises dashi – Japanese stock made with seaweed and dried fish flakes. You can buy instant dashi in Asian food shops, but it's easier to make your own if you're shopping at mainstream supermarkets where the component ingredients seem to be more readily available than the finished product.

For the stock
10g kombu seaweed (kelp)
10g bonito flakes
10g dried shitake mushrooms

100g wheat noodles
1 tbsp soy
1 tbsp mirin
1 slice ginger, matchsticked
3 spring onions, sliced
1 tsp sweet light miso (readily available in supermarkets, Clearspring is a common and good brand)
100g fresh shitake mushrooms, finely sliced
100g oyster mushrooms, larger ones sliced or torn
100g enoki mushrooms, base removed and roughly broken up
1 tsp chopped chives

First make the dashi stock. Place the kombu in a pan, cover with 800ml water and slowly heat. Remove the kombu just before it comes to the boil. Add the bonito flakes and dried mushrooms and simmer for a minute before turning off the heat and leaving to infuse for 15 minutes. Strain the stock.

Next, prepare the noodles according to the packet instructions.

Bring 800ml dashi stock to a simmer. Add the soy, mirin, ginger, spring onions and miso and cook for 2 minutes. Stir in the mushrooms and bring to the boil, then reduce to a simmer and cook for a further 2 minutes. Divide the noodles between two bowls and pour over the broth. Scatter the chopped chives over the top.

Perfect chicken soup with barley

Chicken soup is a subject that inspires much debate, so it makes sense to turn to someone who has done some serious research into it. My good friend Felicity Cloake is the author of the *Guardian*'s Perfect column, for which she's tasked with finding out about the very best version of a dish by assessing some of the top contributions to the culinary sphere, then creating her own.

This is a subtle soup – essentially a stock – and quite brilliant. Each spoonful is so gently nourishing that I find an empty bowl seems to coincide with me feeling energised and uplifted. The idea for using wings comes from Heston, and it's a winner. I have slightly adapted Felicity's recipe.

500g chicken wings
1 bay leaf
1 bunch parsley, leaves and
    stalks separated
1 onion
2 celery sticks
2 carrots
2 leeks
50g pearl barley, rinsed

Put the chicken wings in a pan and add 1 litre cold water, which should just cover them if they're snugly packed in the bottom. Bring to the boil and skim off the scum from the top; this is important – left, it will give the finished soup a greasy, unpleasant flavour.

Add another litre of cold water, along with the bay leaf and parsley stalks, then roughly chop the onion, celery sticks, a carrot and a leek, and tip them in. Season with pepper. Simmer very gently with a lid on for about 2 hours.

Remove the pan from the heat and strain the broth through a fine sieve. Take out the wings and shred the meat off. Place the broth back on the hob with the rinsed barley and bring to the boil. Cook until the barley is soft – about 30 minutes. Finely shred the remaining carrot and leek using a mandolin if you have one, adding them to the broth for the last few minutes. Season very well – chicken soup takes more salt than you'd think; add the shredded chicken and top with a generous scattering of parsley leaves.

Prawn & peanut laksa

This laksa, made with a combination of coconut milk and water, is lighter than a laksa would usually be, which I prefer. It's worth investing in some shrimp paste, as a tiny speck of the stuff gives real depth. If you don't have it, half a minced anchovy will do something similar.

For the laksa paste

1 green bird's eye chilli, seeds removed
1 large shallot
1 large garlic clove
2cm root ginger
1 tsp coriander seeds
1 tsp cumin seeds
1 tsp turmeric
2 tsp peanut butter
1 tsp shrimp paste
Juice of half a lime, plus a squeeze
1 tbsp groundnut oil

For the soup

400g raw prawns
400ml can coconut milk
300-400ml coconut water
1 small sweet potato (100g), diced in 1cm pieces
80g noodles
¼ cucumber, sliced in rounds then quartered
50g bean sprouts

To serve

dry-roasted peanuts
several leaves each of basil, mint, coriander
½ green bird's eye chilli, finely sliced
1 spring onion, finely sliced
½ lime, cut into wedges

First make your laksa paste by blitzing everything in a mini blender. Remove a heaped tsp of the paste and place it in a sandwich bag with the prawns, and an extra squeeze of lime juice. Leave them to marinate for half an hour if you have time, or just while you gather the other ingredients if not. Heat a saucepan over a medium-high heat and cook the remaining paste off for a couple of minutes, using a wooden spoon to stir it around the pan.

Add all the coconut milk and 300ml coconut water to the pan and bring to the boil. Put in the sweet potato and simmer until it is cooked through. Add the remaining 100ml coconut water if you would like your soup a little thinner. Prepare the noodles according to the packet instructions, then put them in the bowls along with the sliced cucumber and bean sprouts. Place another frying pan on the hob and, when hot, quickly fry the prawns until they are pink and crispy.

Pour the broth over the noodles, then top with the prawns, peanuts, herbs, chilli and spring onions. Serve with lime wedges.

Rainbow miso

At its simplest, miso is a Japanese seasoning paste produced by fermenting soybeans, but the amount of soybeans used and other ingredients added can vary considerably. Of the myriad versions available, light and dark are the most common, the former being sweet and mainly comprised of rice and barley and the latter soybean-heavy and aged for longer. This recipe utilises both. If you only have one type, don't worry – just be aware that the dark is stronger, saltier and more savoury than the light variety and adapt the recipe accordingly. I've used freekeh here, an earthy, smoky grain that adds to the robust meatiness of this vegetable soup.

Quick stock suggestion:
1.5 litres water, celery, bay, thyme, lemon peel, parsley, spring onion (see p13)

1 carrot
1 red pepper
1 courgette
1 tbsp olive oil
1 small onion, diced
1 celery stick, diced
2 tbsp dark miso paste
50g freekeh, well rinsed
800ml stock

To serve
2 tbsp natural yoghurt
1 tsp light miso paste
lemon juice, to taste
chives

Prepare the veg for the soup: slice the carrot, pepper and courgette in half; finely dice half of each and use a peeler or a mandoline to thinly slice the rest.

Heat the oil in a saucepan and sweat the onion, celery and other finely chopped veg gently until soft – about 10 minutes. Add the dark miso, freekeh and stock and bring to the boil. Reduce the heat and simmer until the freekeh is cooked – this should take about 30 minutes. Check the seasoning and add the raw thinly sliced veg to the soup and give them a minute to heat through before serving.

Make the miso yoghurt garnish by mixing all of the ingredients together and seasoning. Dollop onto the soup and top with snipped chives.

Watercress & five-spice pork

While the British and French like to blanch and blitz this wonder leaf, the Chinese prefer to slow-cook it – usually with pork ribs – in order to extract nutrients. My take is a blend of Asian flavours and European haste. This recipe doesn't take very long, but it does have several stages so make sure everything is ready before you start.

200g pork tenderloin/pork medallions

For the marinade
1 tbsp light soy sauce
1 tbsp groundnut oil
½ tsp chopped root ginger
small garlic clove
2 spring onions, roughly chopped
1 tbsp rice vinegar
1 green bird's eye chilli, seeds removed
½ tsp five spice

For the soup
100g egg noodles
2 poached eggs
1 tbsp light soy
½ tsp honey
pinch ground white pepper and salt
1 spring onion, finely shredded
1 slice ginger, finely sliced into sticks
200g watercress, thick stalks removed (not necessary with watercress that comes in a salad bag)

Slice the pork into 2cm-thick rounds and place it in a large sandwich bag. Put all the marinade ingredients in a mini blender or finely grate and chop them by hand. Add the mixture to the sandwich bag, massage into the meat and leave for at least 30 minutes (you could leave it overnight but would need to reduce the rice vinegar by half).

Next prepare the noodles as per packet instructions. Rinse them well under cold running water and set them aside. Time to poach your eggs. I prefer the Heston method, which doesn't require using any vinegar or creating a whirlpool in the saucepan. Simply crack your egg into a sieve to strain away the part of the white that would form straggly bits if cooked. Now tip it into water that has been brought to the boil but is now just simmering. Cook according to preference, usually about 4 minutes.

Add 600ml water to a saucepan along with the soy, honey, salt and pepper, spring onion and ginger and bring to the boil, then simmer for 5 minutes. Heat a griddle pan till it's smoking and cook the pork medallions for 2-3 minutes each side – or until cooked to taste. Slice the meat into strips. Plunge the watercress into the hot liquid and cook for another 30 seconds, or until it is just wilted. To serve, divide the noodles between two bowls and top with the broth, pork and poached eggs.

Tamarind & tomato

Known as *rasam*, this thin soup is India's answer to Thailand's *tom yum* – it's thirst-quenching and medicinal and takes mere minutes to pull together. Be warned that all tamarind pulp is not equal, and I would avoid the paste you get in supermarket jars as this contains a host of other ingredients that seem to dull tamarind's sticky, sour-tasting vibrancy. What you want is a block of tamarind pulp, which is made of 100% shelled tamarind fruit. It's available from Asian shops and some well-stocked supermarkets, but the easiest thing is to buy it online where the choice is large. Don't be put off by all of the stages listed below. None of them take too long.

60g dried tamarind pulp

For the spice mix
2 tsp cumin seeds, toasted
1 tsp black peppercorns
2 garlic cloves
1 small bunch coriander, stalks only, leaves added just before serving
¼ tsp turmeric

For the soup
1 tbsp coconut oil
1 tsp mustard seeds
1 green bird's eye chilli, split lengthways
10 fresh curry leaves
500g tomatoes, a combination of cherry and large, halved and quartered

First you'll need to prepare your tamarind. Place it in a bowl and cover it with 200ml boiling water. Leave it for 5 minutes, then massage it until it dissolves and you have a thickened liquid. Push the liquid through a sieve to remove the seeds, then set aside.

Using either a small blender or a pestle and mortar, crush the cumin, peppercorns, garlic and coriander stalks. Mix in the turmeric and set aside.

Heat the oil in a saucepan and put in the mustard seeds, chilli and curry leaves, stirring until the mustard seeds start popping. Stir in the tomatoes, followed by the spice mix and cook for another couple of minutes. Then add half the tamarind pulp and 500ml water. Bring to the boil and cook for 5 minutes. Season generously with salt, then taste and add more tamarind pulp if you'd like more tang. Stir in the coriander leaves before serving.

A selection of wholesome
soups that verge on being
stews. They're packed full
of pulses, spices and
protein, everything you
need for the daily battle.

quick

raw

slow

broth

hearty

soup

African peanut

Peanut butter is an important ingredient in this soup, so make sure you opt for a good quality one made of just roasted peanuts and a pinch of sea salt, and not padded out with palm oil. Alternatively, make your own by blitzing some briefly roasted skinned peanuts in a blender along with a pinch of salt. It really is that easy.

The scotch bonnet is an exceptionally hot chilli so the safest way to use it is to pierce the skin all over with a sharp knife before adding it to your soup. This should give a mild spice. However, if you're after something a little more fiery, simply knock the cooked chilli against the side of the saucepan with the back of a wooden spoon and you'll be amazed at the heat that comes out.

1 tbsp groundnut oil
1 small onion, finely chopped
1 red pepper, finely chopped
1 celery stick, finely chopped
1 garlic clove, chopped
5 large tomatoes (500g), chopped
1 small sweet potato (100g), peeled and grated
1 sprig thyme, leaves only
1 tsp red wine vinegar
100g peanut butter
2 tbsp tomato purée
900ml water or stock
1 scotch bonnet pepper, whole and pricked
20g rice (optional)
handful peanuts, to serve

Heat the oil in a saucepan with a large base, then add the onion, red pepper, celery, garlic, tomatoes, sweet potato and thyme and cook for 10 minutes, or until everything has softened. Stir in the red wine vinegar, peanut butter and tomato purée, making sure the peanut butter, in particular, is well mixed in and there are no lumps. Cook for another couple of minutes before pouring in the water or stock along with the scotch bonnet. If you are using rice, add it at this stage. Bring to the boil and then simmer for at least 30 minutes. Season well with salt and pepper and top with peanuts for added crunch.

This is a plentiful soup for two without the optional rice, so know that adding it will make it very generous indeed, or enough to serve three.

Ginger congee with mackerel & sesame

Congee is rice porridge and therefore falls into the category of breakfasts that also make good dinners. It is a soup served to the sick in both Japan and China because rice that has been cooked until it dissolves is unsurprisingly very easy to digest. Depending on where you are in Asia, congee can vary from being a thin broth to a much thicker soup (the category mine falls into). Regardless of these differences, jasmine rice is essential as it's quicker to lose its shape than other less glutinous types, while also being nutty and distinctly fragrant.

80g jasmine rice
3cm root ginger, sliced into matchsticks
2 garlic cloves, finely chopped
1 tbsp bonito flakes (optional)
1 litre water

For the topping
1 tsp groundnut oil
1 leek, sliced into thin rounds
1 carrot, thinly sliced using a peeler (or spiralised/julienned if you have the gadgets to hand)
2 lumps stem ginger, thinly matchsticked, plus 1 tsp syrup
2 smoked mackerel fillets, flaked
lime juice, to taste
1 tsp sesame seeds
1 tsp sesame oil
handful coriander leaves, to serve
bonito flakes (optional), to serve

Cover the rice with lots of water in a big bowl and swish it about with your hand to give it a good clean. Drain it through a sieve and repeat one more time. Put the drained rice in a saucepan with the ginger, garlic, a pinch of salt, bonito flakes (if using) and the water. Bring to the boil, then cover and simmer for an hour, or until all of the rice grains have disintegrated. Stir the pot vigorously whenever you happen to be passing to help the rice grains break down. When you're ready to serve, loosen the congee with around 100ml boiling water. Check the seasoning.

To make the mackerel topping, heat the oil in a frying pan and add the leek and carrot. Continue cooking until the veg are tender and lightly browned. Turn the heat off and add the stem ginger pieces and syrup, flaked mackerel, lime juice, sesame oil and seeds. Season with salt and pepper and give it a good stir.

Top the congee with the mackerel mix and scatter over the coriander leaves. You may want to adjust the flavouring by adding some extra stem ginger syrup, lime juice and sesame oil. Some extra bonito flakes sprinkled on top would be a nice addition if you're using them.

Beer & bread

One for severe weather conditions, this is the sort of soup that immediately ignites a fire in your belly and turns your cheeks red. It's taken from Lizzie Kamenetzky's book *Winter Cabin Cooking* and is a speciality of the Valais region of the Swiss Alps. In her words: 'The hoppy flavour of the beer mingles with the deep richness of the rye bread. You can use any type of mountain cheese, such as Comté or Gruyère but raclette cheese adds its own unique flavour to the soup.'

300g rye bread, cut into cubes
330ml beer (lager or golden beer)
330ml fresh beef stock
good glug of double cream, to taste
handful chives, finely snipped
40g raclette cheese, cut into little cubes

Soak the bread in the beer for half an hour then blend into a smooth mixture. Heat the beef stock, add the bread and beer and simmer for 15-20 minutes. Stir in the cream and chives and serve in warm bowls scattered with the little pieces of cheese.

Bengali-spiced fish

This soup relies on the spice carom, otherwise known as *ajwain*, *ajwan* or *ajowan*. The seeds look like a stubby version of cumin or caraway, but they have a little tail and an aroma closer to dried thyme. It's a spice commonly used in Ayurvedic medicine, considered a powerful cleanser and imbued with lots of digestive properties. Its flavour is all its own and it's utterly delicious – just half a teaspoon imparts a strong flavour. It's available in Asian shops, health food shops and bigger supermarkets, as well as online, under all of the names given above.

1 tbsp groundnut oil
2 garlic cloves, chopped
½ tsp carom seeds
1 bay leaf
1 small onion, finely chopped
400ml can coconut milk
400ml fish stock
pinch salt
1 green finger chilli, split
  lengthways
¼ tsp turmeric
40g rice
2 tsp grainy mustard
300g haddock, skin removed
  but left as intact as possible
50g frozen peas

Heat the oil in a wide-based pan. Add the garlic, carom seeds and bay, and heat until the seeds begin to crackle. Stir in the onion and sauté it for several minutes before adding the coconut milk, stock, salt, chilli, turmeric and rice. Bring to the boil, then reduce to a simmer and cook for 15 minutes, or until the rice is tender. Stir the mustard in and mix thoroughly. Poach the fish in the soup – this should take about five minutes. The fish is cooked as soon as it starts to look opaque and flakes apart when pushed. Add the peas 4-5 minutes before the end of cooking.

Fish chowder with crispy capers

2 tbsp capers
1 tbsp olive oil, plus more
   to fry capers
1 leek, finely sliced
2 garlic cloves, chopped
2 sprigs thyme, leaves only
1 bay leaf
1 tbsp plain flour (optional)
200g new potatoes, quartered
500ml milk
200ml water/fish stock
4 sprigs tarragon, leaves only,
   roughly chopped (handful
   reserved for garnish)
1 tbsp Dijon mustard
2 tbsp crème fraiche
400g mixed fish (salmon,
   haddock, cod), skinned and
   cut into 3cm chunks
½ lemon, juice and zest
dash Tabasco

For the capers
2 tbsp capers
Oil to fry

It's the fried capers that really make this chowder, providing crispy little croutons. Although the smaller peppercorn-sized 'nonpareille' capers are considered to have the best flavour, the bigger ones burst better in this instance, making the rather dramatic transformation into flowers. A poached egg would be a welcome addition to this soup – for a good poaching method see page 106. This chowder is best eaten on the day it's made.

Drain and rinse your capers under cold water, then dry them thoroughly with paper towels and set them aside. Heat the oil and cook the leek, garlic, thyme and bay over a very low heat for about 5 minutes. Add the flour and cook for 2 minutes, then the potatoes and cook for another 2 minutes. Pour in the water or stock together with most of the tarragon and bring gently to the boil. Immediately reduce to a gentle simmer (this is important with milk – it can curdle if you boil it) and cook until the potatoes are done.

Heat a centimetre of oil in a small saucepan, and fry the capers for about 2 minutes. They should burst open and go slightly brown. Remove them with a slotted spoon and drain them on paper towels. (They lose their crispiness after an hour or so, so make them just before serving.)

Add the mustard, crème fraîche and plenty of black pepper to the soup, stir thoroughly, then place the fish on top of everything and continue to cook on a medium heat for about 6-8 minutes, or until the fish flakes apart when pushed. Turn the heat off and add the lemon juice, zest and a dash of Tabasco a little at a time to taste, stirring gently to incorporate. Divide the chowder between two bowls then sprinkle over the crispy capers and the rest of the tarragon.

Romanian fisherman's soup

This is a simple sour soup, which tastes far better than you'd expect from the sum of its parts. There's a reason why every Romanian who decamps to the banks of the Danube for the summer eats this every day. It's traditionally composed of whatever freshwater fish is available – sturgeon, pike, carp and catfish, the more varieties the better – and water straight from the Danube, which has a soft buttery quality. As I don't have Danube water to hand, I finish my soup with a little melted butter. This soup is best eaten on the day it's made.

1 tbsp olive oil
1-3 waxy potatoes (depending on size), thinly sliced
1 onion, sliced
1 carrot, cut in rounds
1 red pepper, sliced
1 celery stick, sliced, leaves reserved for garnish
small bunch parsley, stalks finely chopped, leaves reserved
small bunch coriander, stalks finely chopped, leaves reserved
1 tbsp tomato paste
1 litre water/fish stock
8 cherry tomatoes, halved
250g meaty fish fillet(s)
small bunch dill, finely chopped
2 tbsp lemon juice

To serve
1 tbsp melted butter (optional)
bread
garlic aioli
extra lemon juice, to taste

Heat the oil in a pan and sweat the first five ingredients along with the parsley and coriander stalks for 10 minutes. Add the tomato purée and cook for another 2 minutes. Pour in the water with the tomatoes and simmer until the potatoes are cooked. Poach the fish fillet(s) gently in the soup, stirring to break them up. Season very well and stir in the dill, the reserved parsley and coriander leaves and the lemon juice. This should be quite a sour soup, so serve with extra lemon to taste.

Drizzle a little melted butter over each bowl and eat with bread and garlic aioli.

Shaksoupa

Thanks must go to Ottolenghi for giving this gem of a dish a makeover in the last couple of years. Once confined to being a North African and Israeli brunch, shakshuka now makes regular appearances on restaurant menus and home dinner tables. It is a simple dish that involves poaching eggs in a frying pan of thick spiced tomato and red pepper sauce. Because my version is a soupier affair I find it easier to poach my eggs separately and add them, but you could cook them in the soup if you prefer.

Quick stock suggestion:
1.5 litres water, carrot, garlic, celery, thyme, bay, parsley stalks, peppercorns, a dried chilli, lemon peel (see p13)

½ tsp cumin seeds
½ tsp paprika
½ tsp ground cumin
½ tsp ground coriander
½ tsp cinnamon
¼ tsp turmeric
1 tbsp olive oil
1 red onion, finely diced
2 garlic cloves, sliced
2 sprigs thyme, leaves only
1 tbsp tomato purée
½ tbsp red wine vinegar
1 red pepper, chopped into 1cm pieces
500g tomatoes, half large, half cherry, all diced into 1cm cubes
800ml water/stock

To serve
2 eggs
pinch pink peppercorns, crushed
pinch sumac
parsley, chives, snipped

Place a saucepan over a medium heat and dry-fry the cumin seeds for 2 minutes, stirring frequently, before adding the rest of the spices. Cook for another minute or so, then add the oil and chopped onion, turn the heat to low and sweat for 5 minutes. Stir in the garlic, thyme leaves, tomato purée and red wine vinegar and cook for 5 minutes. Next add the chopped red pepper and tomatoes, turn the heat up and cook until the red veg slightly collapse, about 5 minutes. Now add the water or stock and bring to the boil, then reduce the heat and simmer for 30 minutes. Season with salt and pepper.

While the soup is cooking, poach your eggs. I prefer the Heston method, which doesn't require using any vinegar or creating a whirlpool in the saucepan. Simply crack your egg into a sieve to strain away the part of the egg white that would form straggly bits if cooked. Now tip it into water that has been brought to the boil but is now just simmering. Cook according to preference – I usually go for 4 minutes. Serve with pinches of crushed pink peppercorns and sumac and chopped-up parsley and chives. You could also add some crumbled feta, olives or even the finely shredded skin of a preserved lemon if you happen to have a jar in the fridge.

Sweet potato with grated ginger & paprika oil

Ginger sings when it's generously grated on top of this soup. Use as much as you can take. Arm yourself with a grating implement that's up to the task (a microplane would be my choice), as this knobbly root has a relentlessly fibrous texture. The fresher the ginger, the juicier and easier to grate.

Quick stock suggestion:
1.2 litres water, onion, celery, carrot, bay, thyme, garlic (see p13)

For the soup
400g sweet potatoes
1 tbsp olive oil
1 onion, diced
1 celery stick
1 garlic clove
600ml stock/water

For the paprika oil
1 tsp paprika
1 tbsp olive oil

To serve
2 tbsp crème fraîche
2cm root ginger, grated

Preheat the oven to 190°C/170°C fan. Prick the sweet potatoes and bake them whole for about 45 minutes, or until they are very soft. If your potatoes are quite large, you could cut them in half lengthways and put them on the baking tray cut side down to reduce the cooking time. When they are done, scoop out the flesh.

To make the paprika oil, heat the paprika in a dry pan over a medium heat, gently stirring it with a wooden spoon until it releases its aroma (a minute or so). Then add the oil to the pan and mix it well. Immediately transfer it to a small bowl and allow the sediment to settle at the bottom. The oil will taste best if it's given time to infuse, so leave it for anything from half an hour to overnight.

For the soup, heat the oil in a saucepan and sweat the onion and celery over a very low heat until soft – about 10 minutes. Add the garlic and cook for a further 2 minutes before adding the sweet potato flesh and the stock or water. Bring to the boil, then simmer for 5 minutes. Blitz it all in a blender and adjust the seasoning.

Serve with crème fraîche, plenty of freshly grated ginger and a drizzle of paprika oil.

The great chorizo cure

With its frilly leaves curly kale is tremendously adept at cradling rivulets of tasty liquid, which makes its inclusion in richly flavoured soups and stews wise. Back before kale became a thing, my brother and sister and I used to grow it in a veg trug on a patch of pavemented garden in London, and it grew so fast and so rampantly that for a time we ate this Spanish-style soup almost daily. I wouldn't call it a cleansing soup, but there's something incredibly healing about a deep red pot of sausagey stew that's been generously watered with wine – it seems to cure all.

1 tbsp olive oil
200g raw cooking chorizo, sliced into 2cm discs
1 bushy sprig rosemary, leaves only, roughly chopped
2 garlic cloves, thinly sliced
1 onion, finely chopped
¼ tsp paprika
120ml red wine
400g can tinned cherry tomatoes
400g can chickpeas
1 can water
100g kale, tough stalks removed

Heat the oil, and fry the chorizo over a high heat until it releases its oil. Reduce the heat and add the rosemary, garlic, onion and paprika. Sweat them together for 10 minutes. Turn the heat back up and pour in the red wine, allowing it to burn off for a minute before adding the tinned tomatoes, drained chickpeas and water. Bring to the boil, then reduce the heat and simmer for 30 minutes. Taste and adjust the seasoning. When all the flavours have melded, push the kale beneath the surface of the liquid and cook it for a further 10 minutes, or until it's soft.

Piccalilli

Luridly coloured and bizarrely named, piccalilli is an odd condiment, composed of little pieces of pedestrian vegetables generously coated in turmeric and mustard. Despite its Indian aspirations, it's very much a British food, traditionally served alongside crumbly wedges of Cheddar and cold meats, and while its curiously jovial name remains a mystery, it's a pleasure to say. This soup turns what is usually an accompaniment into the main event, a position I think it's well suited for.

Quick stock suggestion:
1.2 litres water, onion, celery, carrot, bay, garlic (see p13)

30g butter
1 small onion, finely chopped
1 celery stalk, finely chopped
1 carrot, finely chopped
1 small cauliflower (400g), broken into florets, stalks finely chopped
1 garlic clove, chopped
1 tart green apple, peeled and grated
1 tbsp cider vinegar
1 tbsp honey (or more to taste)
½ tsp black mustard seeds
½ tsp yellow mustard seeds
1 tsp turmeric
1 tsp ground cumin
½ tsp mustard powder
600ml water/stock
1 green finger chilli, split lengthways
handful green beans, sliced into 2cm pieces
Cheddar, to serve

Melt the butter in a saucepan and sweat together the onion, celery, carrot and cauliflower stalks (the florets will be added later) for 10 minutes, or until soft. Then add the garlic, apple, vinegar, honey and spices and cook for 2 minutes. Pour in the water or stock with the green chilli. and simmer for 20 minutes. Remove from the heat and use a stick blender to partially blend.

Return the soup to the heat, bring it back to the boil and add the reserved cauliflower florets and sliced green beans. Cook for 2 minutes, or until the vegetables are done to your liking. Taste and adjust the seasoning.

Serve a good wedge of Cheddar alongside; alternatively, grate it directly into the soup.

Ris e bisi with tarragon oil

This traditional Venetian dish falls somewhere between a risotto and a soup, depending on who makes it. My version is firmly in the soup category, naturally. It's particularly delicious made with a good chicken stock, and if you're using fresh peas, tossing some pods into a quick vegetable stock will give great results too. Having said that, it's fairly forgiving so an instant stock will be fine. I've included a recipe for tarragon oil, which goes very well with this risotto, but so will parsley oil or basil oil – either, or a mixture, using the method below.

Quick stock suggestion:
1.5 litres water, onion, carrot, celery, garlic, Parmesan rind, pea pods

For the soup
2 tsp olive oil
1 tsp butter
1 onion, finely chopped
1 celery stick, finely chopped
1 garlic clove, chopped
100g risotto rice
700ml stock
200g frozen peas
2 tbsp grated Parmesan
handful pea shoots

For the herb oil
1 small bunch tarragon, leaves removed
2 tbsp oilve oil
sea salt

Melt the oil and butter in a pan and cook the onion and celery over a low heat for about 10 minutes. Add the rice and garlic and stir to coat with the vegetables and oil, then pour in the stock and bring to the boil. Reduce to a simmer and cook for 15 minutes. Put in the frozen peas, bring back to the boil and simmer for another 5 minutes. Stir in half of the Parmesan and check the seasoning.

To make the herb oil, first find a bowl big enough to fit your sieve inside it. Put a handful of ice in the bowl and cover with water. Keep this next to the sink. Place the tarragon leaves in a sieve held over the sink and pour freshly boiled water over them until they wilt. Immediately plunge the same sieve into your bowl of iced water to refresh the leaves. Then lift it out of the water and push the leaves against it to drain. Blend with olive oil until smooth, then strain through a sieve and season with sea salt.

Serve the soup with a drizzle of the herb oil, and topped with the pea shoots and remaining Parmesan.

bread

Breads that don't contain yeast and therefore arrogantly bypass any associated kneading and resting. Simply mix your ingredients and bake.

Cornbread

I was making cornbread in a very different way before I tasted chef Brad McDonald's recipe, served at his restaurant The Lockhart in London. Other recipes are rendered obsolete once you've tried it. Make sure you get your hands on the coarsest polenta available, as this is key to achieving the most satisfying granular texture. Brad uses a bit of pork fat to glaze the cake tin before adding the batter; if you'd like to include this step you can pick up a little from your butcher. He also uses 20g more sugar than I've called for and serves it with some softened butter and a little honey or maple syrup. Even without these tasty additions, it's pretty special.

150g coarse yellow polenta
150g plain flour
30g soft light-brown sugar
1 tsp baking powder
1 tsp salt
2 large eggs, lightly beaten
240ml milk
30g butter, melted and cooled

Preheat the oven to 210°C/190°C fan. Grease a 20cm cake tin with a little butter and set it aside while you make the cornbread batter.

In a bowl, mix together the dry ingredients. Mix the eggs and milk in a jug. Just before you mix the dry and wet ingredients, place your greased cake tin in the oven to heat up. Make a well in the centre of the dry ingredients and gradually pour in the wet ones. Finally add the melted butter, and gently fold it through.

Take your cake tin out of the oven and pour in the batter. Bake for 20 to 25 minutes, or until a skewer inserted into the centre of the bread comes out clean.

Seeded buckwheat loaf

A powerhouse of seeded goodness and a highly addictive nutty loaf to boot. Half of the seeds and nuts are ground to flour in this recipe – meaning that they're easier for your stomach lining to absorb – while the other half are left intact to give texture. The seeds and flour are gluten-free, but make sure you also use gluten-free oats if you're making it for anyone with coeliac disease. Psyllium husks are essential – they're a binder and keep the whole thing together in lieu of gluten – and they're easy to find in health food shops.

100g sunflower seeds
100g pumpkin seeds
50g whole almonds
50g linseeds (or flaxseeds)
50g jumbo oats
100g buckwheat flour
4 tbsp psyllium seed husks
¾ tsp fine salt
350ml water

Take half of each of the first four ingredients (50g each of the sunflower and pumpkin seeds and 25g each of the almonds and linseeds) and put them in a powerful blender. Blitz to a flour, then place them in a large bowl with the rest of the ingredients, except the water. Make a well in the centre of the mix and pour in the water, using a wooden spoon to gradually introduce the dry mix to the wet. Make sure everything is fully incorporated, then leave aside for about 30 minutes to an hour. When you come back to the mix, which you were just able to wade a wooden spoon through before, it will be so stiff that it will resemble day-old porridge. Push the dough into a greased 500g loaf-tin and level it out, then top it with a decorative sprinkling of extra seeds.

Preheat the oven to 180°C/160°C fan, and bake the loaf for 1 hour. Then remove it carefully from its tin and place it back on the shelf for another 15-30 minutes. The loaf is ready when a skewer comes out without any goo (it can still be a little wet – this loaf tends to be until it's had time to cool). Remove it from the oven and allow it to cool on a rack. This bread is equally delicious eaten as it is or toasted. It also freezes brilliantly.

Everyday wholemeal soda

Soda bread takes very little time to prepare. The most challenging part is sourcing buttermilk before you begin; whereas it's available on every corner in Ireland, only the bigger supermarkets seem to sell it in England. Soda bread is best eaten on the day it is baked, and freezes well too. Slice up and freeze anything you don't eat straightaway and defrost a slice at a time to accompany soup or to toast. It would be sad to eat soda bread without butter.

300g stoneground wholemeal
   flour
300g plain flour
1 tsp salt
1 tsp bicarbonate of soda
400ml buttermilk

Preheat the oven to 200°C/180°C fan. Mix the dry ingredients together in a large bowl. Make a well in the centre and pour in the buttermilk. Working from the centre, gradually introduce more flour. Knead lightly until the dough comes together. If it is sticky add a tiny bit more plain flour. Transfer the dough to a lined baking sheet, shape it into a round and flatten it slightly. With a knife, mark a deep cross in the top of the loaf. Bake it in the oven for 45 minutes to 1 hour, or until the bread looks cooked at the apex of the cross you made, and the underside sounds hollow when tapped. Transfer it to a wire rack and leave it to cool.

Bentley's soda bread

This is Richard Corrigan's decadent winning take on soda bread, served in his restaurant Bentley's. It is a truly show-stopping loaf. Not only does the treacle add a savoury sweetness, it also turns the loaf the colour of licorice, studded only by jumbo oat flakes. Makes a small loaf.

130g plain flour
130g wholemeal flour (if you use stoneground, or another coarse flour, you may need extra)
1 tsp salt
2 tsp bicarbonate of soda
70g jumbo porridge oats
1 tbsp runny honey
1 tbsp black treacle
250ml buttermilk

Preheat the oven to 200°C/180°C fan. Line a baking sheet with baking parchment. Mix all the dry ingredients together in a bowl. Make a well in the centre and then mix in the honey, treacle and buttermilk, working everything together lightly with your hands, until you have a loose, wet dough. With floured hands, shape the dough into a round and lift on to the lined baking sheet. With a knife, mark a cross in the top.

Bake it in the oven for about 35 minutes, or until the loaf sounds hollow when tapped on the base. Transfer it to a wire rack, drape a damp cloth over the top and leave it to cool.

Index

Acknowledgements

My thanks to Aurea Carpenter, Rebecca Nicolson, Klara Zak and the rest of the excellent team at Short Books. To Georgia Vaux for her design. And to Romas Foord for taking beautiful pictures, and allowing me to make a mess of his kitchen.

Thank you to the cooks who've generously donated delicious recipes: Felicity Cloake, Amy & Julie Zhang, Lizzie Kamenetzky, Richard Corrigan and Brad McDonald. Thank you to Jane Suthering for letting me rifle through her vast library of cookbooks, and to Chris Koury for letting me pick her encyclopaedic brain.

To my friends and family, always on hand to chat soup, sample soups, test soup recipes, give opinions on the naming of soups, or simply relieve me of soups taking up fridge and freezer space: my sister Elizabeth, Margaret, Steph, Polly, Becky, Henri, Jennifer, Naomi, my brothers Michael, Patrick and Conor, and Dad. Special thanks to Phil for suffering soups the most, and to Mum for making me realise early on that the kitchen is the best place to be.

Henrietta Clancy is a cook, food writer and food stylist based in South London. After training at Ballymaloe cookery school and studying English literature at Trinity College in Dublin, she cut her teeth at various food, drink and travel magazines. She now writes and styles for publications including the Guardian, Observer and The Times. She has also run a number of successful pop up restaurants.

Published in 2016 by
Short Books, Unit 316, ScreenWorks, 22 Highbury Grove,
London, N5 2ER

10 9 8 7 6 5 4 3 2 1

Photographs copyright © Romas Foord

A CIP catalogue record for this book
is available from the British Library.

ISBN: 978-1-78072-265-8

Design by Georgia Vaux

Printed in Italy